COPING WITH AN ANXIOUS OR DEPRESSED CHILD

'ou are a parent of an anxious child, or you work with anxious ren, then this book will answer all your questions.'

Dr Charlotte Wilson, University of East Anglia

a time when access to child mental health services is difficult, and e pressures on clinicians' time are higher than ever, this book greatly appreciated both by parents looking for information ractical advice, as well as by child and adolescent mental clinicians looking for a useful resource to recommend to ...lies.'

Dr James Murray, Research Tutor in Psychology,
University of Surrey

vides parents with many practical ideas about how to cope with nxious or depressed child.'

Paul Stallard, Professor of Child & Family Mental Health,
University of Bath

Coping with an
Anxious or Depressed Child
A guide for parents and carers

Sam Cartwright-Hatton

ONEWORLD
OXFORD

COPING WITH AN ANXIOUS OR DEPRESSED CHILD

Published by Oneworld Publications 2007

Copyright © Sam Cartwright-Hatton 2007

ISBN-13: 978–1–85168–482–3
ISBN-10: 1–85168–482–4

Typeset by Jayvee, Trivandrum, India
Cover design by Mungo Designs
Printed and bound by TJ International Ltd., Padstow, Cornwall

Oneworld Publications
185 Banbury Road
Oxford OX2 7AR
England
www.oneworld-publications.com

Learn more about Oneworld. Join our mailing list to
find out about our latest titles and special offers at:

www.oneworld-publications.com/newsletter.htm

Contents

Series Foreword

This series is intended to provide clear, accessible, and practical information to individuals with a wide range of psychological disorders, as well as to their friends, relatives, and interested professionals. As the causes of emotional distress can be complex, books in this series are not designed purely to detail self-treatment information. Instead, each volume sets out to offer guidance on the relevant, evidence-based psychological approaches that are available for the particular condition under discussion. Where appropriate, suggestions are also given on how to apply particular aspects of those techniques that can be incorporated into self-help approaches. Equally important, readers are offered information on which forms of therapy are likely to be beneficial, enabling sufferers to make informed decisions about treatment options with their referring clinician.

Each book also considers aspects of the disorder that are likely to be relevant to each individual's experience of receiving treatment, including the therapeutic approaches of medical professionals, the nature of diagnosis, and the myths that might surround a particular disorder. General issues that can also affect a sufferer's quality of life, such as stigma, isolation, self-care and relationships are also covered in many of the volumes.

The books in this series are not intended to replace therapists, since many individuals will need a personal treatment programme from a qualified clinician. However, each title offers individually tailored strategies, devised by highly experienced practising clinicians, predominantly based on the latest techniques of cognitive behavioural therapy, which have been shown to be extremely effective in changing the way sufferers think about themselves and their problems. In addition, titles also include a variety of practical features such as rating scales and diary sheets, helpful case studies drawn from real life, and a wide range of up-to-date resources including self-help groups, recommended reading, and useful websites. Consequently, each book provides the necessary materials for sufferers to become active participants in their own care, enabling constructive engagement with clinical professionals when needed and, when appropriate, to take independent action.

Dr Steven Jones
Series Editor

1

Is this book for you?

Who is this book for?

This book is aimed at anyone who is bringing up a child who is anxious or depressed. It is most suited to helping children who are up to about fifteen years of age. The book gives guidance on when and how to seek assistance for your child, and advice on how you, as a parent, can help.

What are anxiety and depression?

Anxiety and depression are types of 'emotional disorder'. It used to be believed that children and adolescents did not really suffer from these emotional disorders. However, in the past decade or so there has been a slow realisation that children can and do get these disorders, and when they do it is as unpleasant for them as it is for adults. The symptoms that an anxious or depressed child will experience will be very similar to those that adults get. However, there are one or two additional symptoms that you may see in children more than in adults.

Symptoms of anxiety and depression

The symptoms that may indicate that your child is depressed or has an anxiety disorder are many and varied. Also, every person is different and will have a slightly different set of symptoms. A child does not need to have all of the symptoms before they can get diagnosed with a disorder. Below, I have listed the sorts of symptoms that a child with a formal diagnosis of anxiety or depression will have. However, I would make two notes of caution. First, there is a lot of controversy over what symptoms are and are not required for someone to get a diagnosis of anxiety or depression. If you are worried about your child but they do not totally fit the descriptions given here, please do still go and find help for your child. Secondly, and on the other hand, just because your child seems to have a lot of the symptoms that I describe below, do not assume that they have got a serious diagnosable disorder. Most children and adolescents will show some of the symptoms at some point or other (there is some evidence to suggest that children who have no symptoms are the unusual ones!). Diagnosing these disorders is a complex skill that many highly trained and experienced professionals still struggle with. So, please don't attempt to do any diagnosing yourself (you will only risk needless worry) and, if you are worried about your child, get them some help. Where to go for help is discussed in chapter 4. The list below is just to give you an indication of the sort of symptoms that you can expect to see if you know that you have an anxious or depressed child, and to give some reassurance that some of the bizarre and, frankly, annoying behaviours that they might display are probably part of their anxiety or depression. Remember, even if your child just has one or two symptoms, it is worth seeking help if you are worried.

Box 1.1. Symptoms of anxiety and depression in children and adolescents

Anxiety symptoms

- Feels scared when away from parent – avoids being separated from parent
- Frequent crying
- Frequent worrying about losing parents
- Very worried about doing something embarrassing in public
- Dislikes going to busy places or big gatherings
- Hates being centre of attention
- Has a phobia, e.g. of an animal or insect, blood, getting hurt, the dark, storms, lifts, or something else, that is bad enough that they get very upset and try to avoid the feared object
- Has unexplained physical sensations when scared, e.g. heart racing, sweating, shaking, feeling sick
- Worries about lots of different things, most days
- Finds it hard to stop worrying
- Finds it hard to sleep
- Has lots of aches and pains

Symptoms of depression

- Feels miserable more days than not
- Changes in appetite (it can go up or down with depression)
- Trouble sleeping, or sleeping more than before
- Feels tired and lacking in energy
- Trouble concentrating
- Feels like things are hopeless
- Increased fidgeting
- Can't seem to have fun as much as before
- Is more grumpy than usual
- Thinks about death or dying more than usual

Aren't these just symptoms of teenager disease?

Show this list of symptoms to anyone familiar with teenagers and they will most likely roll their eyes and say, "aren't these just symptoms of being a teenager?" Well, in a way, they have a bit of a point. Many (if not most) teenagers do go through prolonged stages of being grumpy, tired, weepy, eating non-stop, etc. So how do you tell if your child has an emotional disorder, or is simply being a teenager?

If you take your child to see a professional for help with their difficulties, they will ask a number of questions to try to work out whether they need help or not:

- Are the symptoms stopping your child from doing things that they want to do – e.g. are their symptoms stopping them from going out anywhere they like and enjoying themselves, making friends, learning new life skills?
- Are the symptoms stopping your child from doing things that they need to be doing – e.g. going to school, accessing healthcare, learning social skills?
- Are the symptoms impairing family life in any way – e.g. stopping the family from engaging in their normal activities; disrupting normal family routines substantially?
- Are the symptoms posing any physical threat to the child, or to any other person?

If the answer to any of these questions is yes, then it is likely that your child would benefit from some professional help.

Minor differences to the adult conditions

If you are familiar with the adult conditions of anxiety and depression, you may have noticed that the symptoms of the childhood/adolescent disorders are remarkably similar. Most of the symptoms that I have described are also seen in adults who are anxious or depressed. One common difference is the level of grumpiness that you see in depressed children. Depressed adults can get grumpy too, but it seems to be more common in children and adolescents, and can be very difficult for families to cope with.

So are anxious and depressed kids the same as anxious and depressed adults?

There is a lot of overlap between adult depression and anxiety, and child depression and anxiety. Unfortunately, not nearly enough research has been done on child and adolescent emotional disorders, so we don't know much about the subtle differences that might exist between adults and children. In future, it is likely that we will begin to understand more about the differences, but for now, most people see them pretty much the same.

What this book covers

This book is divided into two sections: Section One covers the basic background information that parents with an anxious or depressed child might find helpful. Section Two gives parents some suggestions for helping their anxious or depressed child themselves.

Section One

Chapter 2 talks about how common anxiety and depression are and how likely it is that your child will grow out of it. Chapter 3 moves on to discuss all the different causes of these problems. Most parents want to get hold of some treatment for their children but are bewildered by the remarkable range of treatments (and associated jargon) that is available. Chapter 4 helps parents to navigate this maze, translates some of the jargon, and will help you to find the right person and the right psychological treatment for your child. Chapter 5 talks about medicines that can be prescribed for anxious and depressed children, and talks through the factors that you might want to take into account in deciding whether you want medication for your child. The different medications are described, and there is some information on side effects, and things to watch out for.

Section Two

Section Two of the book moves on to think about what you, as a parent, can do yourself to help your child. Chapter 6 describes some quick and easy basics, including diet and sleep, that can be changed to give your child a boost. Chapter 7 gives some ideas for boosting self-esteem. Chapters 8, 9 and 10 then move on to talk about subtle changes to family life, to the child's environment, and to parenting that can be made to really help the anxious or depressed child to move forward. Chapter 11 focuses on techniques for dealing with your child's worries and fears. Whilst parents are rarely to blame for their child's emotional problems, there are some situations where parents' own problems can spill over into those of their children. Chapter 12 talks about what to do if you suspect that problems of your own, such as mental health problems or marital problems, are impacting on your child's state of mind. Suggestions for when to get help for yourself are given, along with tips for helping to ensure that your problems have a minimal impact on your child's emotional wellbeing. The school environment is very important too, and a supportive school can do wonders for an anxious or depressed child. Chapter 13 gives tips for working with your child's school to the get the best outcome. Chapter 14 briefly rounds up the book, and tells you what to expect in the future.

A note on Obsessive Compulsive Disorder (OCD)

There is another type of anxiety disorder, called Obsessive Compulsive Disorder (OCD), which this book does not specifically cover. This is a condition where the person has frequent unpleasant or distressing thoughts. In order to try to get rid of these thoughts they will engage in rituals, such as frequent washing, cleaning, checking and double checking. Whilst this book contains some general advice that a parent of a child with OCD might find useful, I would strongly suggest that the parent gets professional advice for their child.

SECTION ONE

2

Are anxiety and depression common in childhood, and will they grow out of it?

How common are anxiety and depression in childhood?

Anxiety and depression are surprisingly common in childhood, and even more so in adolescence. Indeed, it is now widely believed that anxiety is the most common psychological disorder of childhood, with depression not far behind. Estimates of how common anxiety and depression are vary hugely depending on which children are being studied, what country they are in, and how the anxiety and depression are measured. However, in one recent and very good study of children in Britain, nearly 4 per cent of children were found to have an anxiety disorder, and nearly 1 per cent of children were found to be clinically depressed. Although this may not sound like very much, it means that in an average school class of thirty children, one or two children will be suffering from anxiety or depression. Indeed, in some other studies, these disorders have been found to be even more common. Also, these studies are just one snapshot taken at one point in time. In studies that have measured children every few years until they are grown up, very many more children have shown up as being anxious or depressed at some point.

Will they grow out of it?

Some children do go through a phase of being really quite anxious, or really quite depressed and then, happily, grow out of it. This is especially true if they just have a mild episode of anxiety or depression. However, for every child who grows out of it, another child will be bothered by bouts of anxiety and depression throughout their life until they get treated. Recent research is even starting to suggest that most adults who are anxious or depressed started to have these problems when they were children or teenagers. For this reason alone, it is worth taking an anxious or depressed child seriously.

Are anxiety and depression harmful for my child?

Some children can get through an emotional disorder without any lasting consequences. However, for the unfortunate ones, having untreated anxiety or depression as a child can leave scars. We know that such children often do not reach their potential at school; it is difficult to concentrate if you are feeling very low, or if your mind is filled with worries. Likewise, childhood should be a time of learning to make friends and learning skills for getting along with other people. We think that some children who are too anxious or depressed to have a full social life miss out on friendships, and miss out on learning the social skills that they will need in later life. Unfortunately, people who enter adulthood without these skills can end up lonely, which leaves them open to even more episodes of anxiety and depression.

Similarly, we suspect that some adolescents who are anxious or depressed can learn to use alcohol, or occasionally street drugs, to help to calm their nerves. In some cases (but by no means all cases), this can lead to problems with alcohol or drugs.

Finally, a note of caution. In rare cases, very depressed children, and sometimes very anxious children, can become so desperate that they can harm themselves and sometimes try to take their own lives. If your child ever gives you reason to think that they may be considering harming themselves, you should talk to your GP as a matter of urgency. If your child ever indicates that they might be thinking of hurting themselves in the near future (i.e. before you can get to the GP), then you should take your child straight to the nearest Accident and Emergency Hospital. Names and addresses of hospitals are in Yellow Pages, the phone directory or on the internet at http://www.nhsdirect.nhs.uk/ or you can call NHS Direct on 0845 4647 and they will tell you where your nearest Accident and Emergency Centre is.

What is the outlook for my child?

Although anxious and depressed children can experience a lot of problems, if they receive good treatment early on, then the outlook is good. Many children and young people who seem very disabled by their emotions can, and do, go on to live happy and fulfilled lives.

Anita was 15 years old when she was referred to CAMHS (Child and Adolescent Mental Health Services). She had refused to go to school for nearly four months, and was almost housebound. Her mother (Sally) was very worried about her and had tried everything that she could think of to get Anita out of the house and to school. None of her cajoling had worked and by now Sally was getting pretty exasperated with Anita. School were threatening to take Sally to

Continued

court because of Anita's absences, and Anita and Sally were barely on speaking terms when they came to their first appointment. At the first appointment it became clear that Anita was suffering from Post Traumatic Stress Disorder (PTSD – a type of anxiety disorder) as a result of some bullying that she had experienced at school. She had become too afraid to go to school and had sat at home brooding and getting very lonely. This had led to depression which, by now, was quite marked. Anita had several months of Cognitive Behaviour Therapy (CBT – see chapter 4), and her mum, Sally, was given some advice in handling this difficult situation. At the end of therapy Anita was back in school (albeit a different school) and was doing very well academically, despite all of the time that she had missed. At the last session, Anita was smiling and relaxed and told her therapist that she was planning to go to sixth form and on to university, which she subsequently did. Although Anita's relationship with her mum was always fiery they had learnt to get along a little better.

In summary, although many children go through periods of feeling anxious about things, and even of feeling pretty miserable, many do go on to do very well. However, those who don't recover completely can experience a lot of misery. Moreover, they can have problems into their adult lives. For these reasons, it is worth getting professional help for your child as soon as possible.

Summary of Chapter Two

➡ **How common are these problems?** Anxiety and depression are very common in children and adolescents, contrary to what was once believed.

➡ **Will my child grow out of this?** Happily, many children will grow out of these problems. However, many will not, and it is always worth seeking treatment.

➡ **Are these things harmful?** Many children are just made unhappy by their anxiety or depression. However, many do suffer serious consequences.

➡ **What is the outlook for my child?** If you get treatment for your child, the outlook is positive.

3

What causes anxiety and depression in children and adolescents?

If I knew the answer to that question, I would probably have a Nobel prize! The most honest answer to this question is that nobody really knows. However, we do have some good ideas about things that make a contribution to our getting anxious or getting depressed. In the vast majority of children it is a combination of lots of things that all add up to making them anxious or depressed. I will go through some of the factors that have been studied in relation to anxiety and depression. If you ever read a book about anxiety and depression in adults, you will read exactly the same things. This is because, as I have mentioned in chapter 1, we do not think that there is much difference between the child and adult versions of these disorders.

Genetics and personality

We know that our genes play a big role in whether we are likely to get anxious or depressed. Some people are just born confident and outgoing, and seem to be able to take life's ups and downs, even if they have had difficult lives that would seem sure to give them problems. On the other hand, some people seem to have great lives where everything is in their favour – lovely family, success at school, lots of friends and plenty of money – and yet they still suffer with anxiety or depression. The fact is, these people were probably made differently from the start. We know from studies looking at children who have been adopted that if your birth mum and dad were prone to anxiety and depression, then you are a bit more likely to get anxious and depressed yourself – even if you have never met your birth mum and dad, and even if you are brought up in a happy and confident adoptive family. However, nothing is guaranteed – far from it. So, even if you have experienced depression or anxiety, it does not mean that your child will definitely go the same way – just that it is a bit more likely for them.

We also know that children are born with their own personality already partially built – and this comes mostly from their genes. We think that some personalities are more prone to becoming anxious or depressed. See the case study below for an example of this.

I have lost count of the number of times that parents have told me the story that appears below – that two children, in

Sarah and Jason were the parents of two children. Their first child, Katie, was easy-going and happy from the moment she was born. She didn't cry too much and she was easily soothed. She seemed to like being in the company of lots of people and adapted easily to changes in her schedule. However, when Joe came along things were very different. Sarah and Jason treated Joe exactly the same way that they had dealt with Katie, but he was just a completely different personality. He cried frequently and was difficult to comfort. He did not like being with strangers and sometimes even struggled when his parents held him. If his routine was changed he did not adapt very easily.

the same family, were completely different from the day that they were born. People used to believe that children were born as 'blank slates' and that all of their personality would be determined by their upbringing. We now know that this is just not true. Children are born with little personalities right from the start. We know that some children are born with sensitive personalities that mean that they are a bit more prone to getting anxious or depressed. Joe was one of these children and he did eventually come to the clinic because of excessive worrying.

Unfortunately, science is not yet advanced enough for us to change our genes. Maybe one day shy, retiring types will be able to pop a pill to change their genes, and overnight they will become the life and soul of the party. However, it is a very long time before that will happen. Fortunately, as we will see, there are lots of other things that go into deciding whether people get anxious or depressed and, unlike changing your genes, these are things that we can actually do something about.

Learning

How do children learn to be adults? It's really quite simple. They do it by watching the adults around them and copying what they do. How many times have you seen your child copying something that you do, or heard them say something using exactly the same words as you?

This amusing story was told to me by one of the mums who came along to our group for parents of anxious children.

Margaret was, by her own admission, a bit of a perfectionist. In particular, she took special pride in her house being spotless and well presented. Once, in an uncharacteristic moment of gossipy-ness, she mentioned to one of her friends that she had been in another friend's bathroom (let's call this friend Beryl) and that it was quite filthy. Margaret's

Continued

> daughter, Claudette, was playing quietly in the corner and appeared to be taking no notice. Taking notice, however, she was. ... Several days later on a trip to Beryl's house, Claudette emerged triumphant from a trip to the lavatory, announcing for all to hear "you're right Mummy, that toilet *IS* filthy" ...!
>
> I asked Margaret what she had learned from this incident, and she said that it had taught her that children copy their parents all the time. She was now very aware that even when Claudette didn't seem to be listening, she was taking in every little thing ...

Clearly in Claudette's situation, she wasn't learning anything too bad. However, if you or anyone who spends a lot of time with your child is ever anxious or depressed, your child could be learning some anxious or depressed behaviours too. We will come back to this idea later.

In particular, there are two types of learning that can teach children anxious or depressive behaviour:

HEARING PEOPLE SAY WORRYING THINGS

When we are running groups for parents of young children, we do a silly exercise where one of us pretends to be a hysterical parent who is too scared to go to the dentist. Much overacting is involved and none of us is ever likely to get an Oscar. There is much shrieking and wailing about how terrible the dentist will be, and how much it will hurt, and "Oh my goodness, the drill!" and so on ... It ends with us picking up the phone and cancelling the dentist appointment. Mostly it just makes the parents in the group laugh, but there is a serious point. After we have done our acting, we ask the parents to say what a young child would have learnt from watching their parent act in this way. They usually say that the child would have learnt that:

• Dentists are nasty
• You should try to not go to the dentist

- Going to the dentist hurts
- Your mum can't cope
- If you are scared, the way to deal with it, is to get all upset and wail and scream and think about the worst possible thing that could happen
- If you are frightened of something, the best thing to do is to stay away from it

All of the research proves that the parents in our group are exactly right. When children hear their parents worrying about something that is scary, they learn to be scared of it too. Also, ask any dentist and they will tell you that they have children coming to see them who are terrified – when they've never even been to the dentist before. These children must have learnt their fear from somewhere.

There are lots and lots of things that children learn from their families. As parents, you are in a really strong position to make sure that your child mostly learns just positive things from you. We will come back to these positive messages later in the book.

LIFE EXPERIENCES

As well as genes and learning, certain life experiences can make some children more vulnerable to anxiety and depression. Mostly, these are life experiences that teach the child that the world is a dangerous place. If a child experiences a serious accident, or is a victim of a violent attack, or sees domestic violence, this can threaten the child's view that the world is a safe place. Instead, they think that the world is dangerous and they can start to watch out for danger. When anyone is on constant red alert for danger, they will become anxious and eventually it will get them down, leading to depression. If your child has experienced or witnessed any traumatic events, this could be one thing that is contributing to their current anxiety/depression. If this has happened, I would strongly advise that you go and talk to your GP as your child may need some special counselling to help them to get over what happened to them. As a parent, there is also a lot that you can do to help your child's world feel safe again. We will come to this later in the book.

However, it doesn't always take a major traumatic event to make a child view the world as a dangerous place. I have seen some sensitive children for whom everyday life stresses can make them feel unsafe. If you are a child whose temperament is a bit sensitive, then you react worse than ordinary children if you get told off too much, if you get smacked, or if your world is a bit unpredictable. In other words, if you just live in an ordinary, busy, stressed-out family (much like we all do), then this can tip you over into being anxious or depressed. However, there is much that parents can do to help a child like this. There are small things about family life that you can change so that your sensitive child copes much better. We will focus on this in Section Two of the book.

Whose fault is it that my child is like this?

It is usually no one's fault. Parents should rarely be blamed for their children's emotional problems. Even if you can see yourself in some of the cases described in this book, you are not to blame for the way your child is. There is no such thing as the perfect parent. What is more, as Sarah and Jason discovered, the same parenting can produce one child who flourishes and another who struggles. Do not feel ashamed that your child has problems. Many parents tell me that they feel embarrassed that other people's children are fine when their child is struggling. However, what they don't realise is that all children are born different and if other people had tried to bring up their child they would probably have found it just as hard.

So, most modern psychologists don't usually blame parents when their children are anxious or depressed. However, although parents don't usually cause these problems, we believe that they can do a lot to help their children get over them.

Summary of Chapter Three

- Anxiety and Depression come from a number of sources:

➡ Genes and personality

Most anxious and depressed people have a genetic make-up that makes them more vulnerable to life's ups and downs. However, even though we can't yet change our genes, there is a lot that parents can do to make their child more resilient.

➡ Learning

Watching how other people deal with stress can teach children to deal with their own stress in a good way or a bad way.

Children easily learn the messages that other people send out about the world – both good and bad.

➡ Life experiences

Seeing or being a victim of a traumatic event (e.g. a serious accident or violence) can make children think that the world is a dangerous place and, in a sensitive child, this can lead to problems. There is much that parents can do to help their child's world feel safe again.

➡ Whose fault is it?

Parents don't usually make their children anxious or depressed, but they are in a great position to help them get better.

4

Psychological treatments for anxious and depressed children

If you have bought this book because you think that your child is anxious or depressed, then I would strongly advise that you go and get some professional advice. You may already have begun this process. In this chapter, I will outline what advice is available, and how you can get hold of it.

Information on different professionals you may come across

There is a whole host of people who work to help children with emotional problems. Although they have different names and different qualifications, you will generally find that their similarities are greater than their differences:

Psychologists

At the moment, anyone can call themselves a psychologist, which is a bit of a problem. If you take your child to see a psychologist in the NHS, you should be fine as their qualifications should have been checked. However, if you go to see someone privately, do take a little care. To be sure that you are getting someone with proper qualifications, ask them whether they are 'chartered'. This means that their qualifications have been checked and approved by the British Psychological Society (BPS). If you have any doubts you can check on the BPS website (see below).

There are three main sorts of psychologist that your child could see: Clinical Psychologists, Counselling Psychologists and Educational Psychologists.

A clinical psychologist will have a psychology degree, followed by some work experience, and then usually a three year postgraduate degree. Most, but not all clinical psychologists have the title "Dr". They will have had specialist training in working with children and adolescents.

A counselling psychologist will have a psychology degree, together with at least a year of postgraduate training. Some counselling psychologists also hold the title "Dr". However, psychologists are not medically qualified. In this country, at least for now, they do not prescribe drugs.

You may also find that you get referred to a "trainee" counselling or clinical psychologist. These people have a psychology degree and are training to become chartered counselling or clinical psychologists. Although they are not yet qualified, they should have an experienced supervisor who closely monitors their work, and you shouldn't feel worried about seeing them; often these most junior members of staff are most up-to-date with the latest research.

You may also come across educational psychologists. Educational psychologists usually work in schools, so if your child is having some difficulties at school, they may get an appointment to see the 'ed psych'. These professionals have a psychology degree and a teaching qualification. They will have taught for a while before doing a one-year professional qualification in school psychology. They usually work with children who are having trouble managing academically at school, or who are having behaviour problems in school. They will sometimes do a bit of one-to-one work with a child, but their main role is to help the school to provide the best support for the child.

Psychiatrists

Psychiatrists are medical doctors who have chosen to specialise in mental health. After four to six years at Medical School and an extra year of general training, they will have specialised in mental health. Psychiatrists come with various different titles which usually tell you how senior they are. A 'Registrar' is a quite junior psychiatrist, but their work will be closely supervised by somebody more senior. A 'Specialist Registrar' or 'SPR' is more senior and, although they are nearly fully qualified, their work will be watched over by a consultant. A 'Consultant' is the most senior psychiatrist. A psychiatrist is, at the moment, the only person that you are likely to see who can prescribe your child any medication. The only exception is your GP or, on occasions, a paediatrician.

Counsellors and Therapists

At the moment, anyone can call themselves a counsellor or a therapist. The counsellors/therapists that you are likely to meet could range from people with very little training and experience to highly trained and skilled professionals. If you get a counsellor/therapist through your GP or hospital, you can be sure that they will have had a minimum level of training. However, if you take your child to see a counsellor privately, take very great care in choosing who you see. At the very least, you should check that your counsellor is registered with the UKCP (see below).

CAMHS Workers and Primary Mental Health Workers

If you get referred to a hospital or clinic, you may well find that you are offered an appointment with a 'Child and Adolescent Mental Health' (CAMHS) Worker or a Primary Mental Health Worker. These people come from a variety of backgrounds, most often social work and nursing. They have chosen to specialise in children's mental health and will have received specialist training in this field.

Psychiatric Nurses

If you get referred to a hospital, you may find that you are offered an appointment with a psychiatric nurse. Psychiatric nurses have usually trained in one of two ways. Many of them began as general nurses working with physical health problems before doing extra training and specialising in mental health. More recently, however, people have been able to train specifically as a mental health nurse without undergoing general nursing training first. In both cases, nurses have received plenty of training and, until they are experienced, they receive lots of supervision of their work.

How to get help

Help from the NHS

You should be able to get help for your child, free of charge, through the NHS. In most cases, the easiest way of doing this is by going along to your GP and explaining your child's symptoms.

However, in some areas you can also get a referral by talking to your school nurse or, very occasionally, by talking to your child's teacher. If you have a health visitor they may also be able to get you a referral.

Help from private sources

In some areas of the country, there are still unacceptably long waiting lists for Child and Adolescent Mental Health Services (CAMHS). Because of this, some parents choose to get private help for their children.

However, for all of the reasons outlined above, do be very careful how you go about doing this. In particular, be very wary of people who advertise solely in telephone directories and newspapers – even if they appear to have a string of qualifications. To be sure that you are getting a minimum level of quality, try to find someone through a professional body such as those described below. This way, you will usually be getting someone with a minimum level of training, and you will be getting someone who has signed up to a set of professional standards in their practice.

If you are looking for help for a child or a young teenager (aged around 15 or less), try to find someone whose listing says that they specialise specifically in work with children and adolescents. Avoid people who seem to claim expertise in lots of other areas too. Working with children is tricky and takes lots of skill and it is unlikely that someone will be sufficiently skilled with children if they work with lots of other different client groups. Ask how much experience your therapist has in working with kids the same age as your child.

SOME GOOD PLACES TO LOOK FOR A PRIVATE PROFESSIONAL ARE AS FOLLOWS:

British Association of Behavioural and Cognitive Psychotherapies (BABCP)

This is the association for professionals who have an interest in cognitive behaviour therapy. As you will see below, cognitive behaviour therapy is highly recommended for treating anxiety and depression in children and teenagers. A list of accredited therapists is available from their website.

Website: http://www.babcp.org.uk/ then click 'find a therapist'. This website has a list of all the professionals who have applied to be registered as Cognitive Behaviour Therapists and who have passed fairly rigorous tests of qualifications, experience, and ongoing supervision. To be on this list, you must be qualified in a caring profession, such as nursing, medicine or clinical psychology (amongst others) and then have done fairly substantial additional training in cognitive behaviour therapy. Not everyone who is qualified to be on this list bothers to register, as you are not required to do so, it takes a lot of time, and they charge a fee. However, if you are looking for a private professional, this is a good place to start. Unfortunately, you will find that very few of those registered as CBT therapists claim to be expert in working just with children and your choice may be a little limited. However, if you are seeking help for an older teenager, many people specialising in work with adults will be happy to see your child and should be equipped to do so.

Cost: At time of going to press, fees vary from £40–£120 per hour.

The British Psychological Society (BPS)

The BPS is the professional society for psychologists working in Britain. At time of going to press, membership is not compulsory and many counselling and clinical psychologists are not registered. However, in the near future, registration will be compulsory for any psychologist who offers services to the public. The BPS website has a list of all of the counselling and clinical psychologists who offer appointments with the public, and states whether these are available privately or just through the NHS.

Website: http://www.bps.org.uk/ then click 'find a psychologist'. This then gives you two choices: the 'directory' of chartered psychologists and the 'register' of chartered psychologists. If you are looking to find a psychologist who can help, use the directory. However, not all psychologists appear in the directory, as you have to pay for your entry. So, if you already have a psychologist in mind, but just want to check that they are qualified, you can check this in the register. The directory is searchable by geographical region, and by speciality – so you are able to search specifically for someone who works with children and adolescents. Everyone who appears on this list will have had their training and qualifications carefully scrutinised, and they agree to adhere to a comprehensive code of practice.

Cost: At time of going to press, fees vary from about £60–£120 per hour.

UKCP

This is the United Kingdom Council for Psychotherapy. All of its members must have minimum levels of training and experience.

Telephone: 0870 167 2131

Website: www.ukcp.org.uk then click 'services', then 'find a therapist'. This section of the website allows you either to find a therapist or to check the registration of one that you have already identified.

Cost: £25–80 approx. per hour, at time of going to press.

BACP

This is the British Association for Counselling and Psychotherapy. All members have a minimum level of training and experience.

Telephone 0870 443 5252

Website: http://www.bacp.co.uk/ then click 'find a therapist'.

Cost: Variable.

What sort of treatment will my child be offered?

Cognitive Behaviour Therapy

Unfortunately, research into the best treatments for anxiety and depression of childhood and adolescence is still·in its fairly early stages. However, since the 1970s, a popular treatment for anxious and depressed adults has been 'Cognitive Behaviour Therapy' or 'CBT'. I will describe what this is in a short while. Hundreds of research trials have shown that cognitive behaviour therapy works well for adults with many types of anxiety and depression, and it is probably about as effective, overall, as medications. In the past decade or so, people have started to look at whether CBT works for children with anxiety or depression. The results have been very good, showing that it probably works about as well for children as it does for adults. In fact, there are very few studies that have tried any other psychological treatments for children and adolescents (there are some drug trials, and I will talk about medications in chapter 5). So, if we are being scientific about things, we should plump for cognitive behaviour therapy every time. Indeed, this is what is starting to happen. The National Institute for Clinical Excellence (NICE) is a British governmental organisation which decides the best treatments for different health problems. They take all of the research, and consult with many different experts in the field, and write a report on what are the best treatments. Basically, they decide what the NHS should be doing. NICE have written a report on how depressed children and teenagers should be treated. Their conclusion was that, if the depression is more than just a passing phase, and more than just a reaction to a bad experience (e.g. bullying), then every child should be offered cognitive behaviour therapy in the first instance. See Box 4.1 for further details.

NICE have not yet written a report on child anxiety but the research evidence for anxiety is very similar to that for

Box 4.1. National Institute for Clinical Excellence: Guidelines for the management of depression in children and adolescents

Initially, for mild depression, one of the following psychological therapies should be offered for a limited period (around 2–3 months): Individual, non-directive, supportive therapy; Group CBT; Guided self help (e.g. information booklets).

If mild depression is unresponsive to one of these therapies after 2–3 months, or if the depression is more severe, then one of the following specific psychological therapies should be offered (for at least 3 months): Individual CBT; Interpersonal therapy; Shorter term family therapy.

If depression is unresponsive to this after four to six sessions, a review should take place, and alternative or additional psychological therapies should be considered, as well as medication. For young people aged 12–18 years, fluoxetine may be offered in addition to psychological therapy; for children aged 5–11 years, the addition of fluoxetine should be cautiously considered.

It is advised that medication should not normally be offered except in combination with psychological therapy. (The use of medication is covered more fully in chapter 5.)

Full details of the NICE guideline are available at: www.nice.org.uk

depression. Basically, cognitive behaviour therapy seems to work quite well for child anxiety and, since there is very little evidence that any other psychological treatments work, cognitive behaviour therapy is probably the best line of attack.

What is Cognitive Behaviour Therapy?

Cognitive behaviour therapy (CBT) aims to help people to change the way that they view themselves and the world. Current thinking suggests that when people are anxious or depressed, it is because they have developed a complex system of beliefs that make them think that the world is dangerous, difficult and unmanageable. If we think these things, then it is not surprising if we feel scared or miserable. It seems that children also have these sets of beliefs, although they may be less crystallised than they are in adults. We know that when we change these beliefs, through the use of cognitive behaviour therapy, people start to feel better. In cognitive behaviour therapy, your child will probably be seen by one therapist who will talk to him/her about their thoughts and feelings about things. The therapist will try to work out if any of these thoughts are causing the anxiety or depression problem, and if so, will work with you and your child to change these. The sort of things that the therapist will ask your child to do is complete fun worksheets, do little experiments to test out whether their thoughts are true or not, and play games to try out new ways of thinking. Often the therapist will ask your child to try new ways of behaving (e.g. going out more) to see if that makes things better. Although some difficult conversations can come up in cognitive behaviour therapy, the aim with children is to try to make the sessions as fun as possible. You may also find, especially with younger children, that the therapist will want to involve you in some sessions. Your child will usually be given tasks to carry out at home, to boost what is being done in the sessions. The therapist may try to enlist your support in making sure that these get done. Your assistance with this can make a real difference between success and failure, although the therapist will want to talk to you about how you can help your child without it feeling intrusive. Typically, the therapist will offer you about six sessions to begin with. After this, you will have a review between yourself, your child and the therapist, and you will decide if there is more to do and whether you would like to have some more sessions. If you carry on, therapy rarely goes on for more than about twenty sessions, unless the problem is very complicated.

Interpersonal Therapy

Interpersonal therapy is an offshoot of cognitive behaviour therapy. It has been found to be useful in some cases of depression where the problem seems to lie in making relationships with other people. It is not widely used in this country. However, if cognitive behaviour therapy is not effective for your child, it might be, as NICE suggest, worth hunting out someone who can do this type of therapy with your child.

Family therapy

As I said above, we don't have much research on what works for childhood anxiety and depression. Very little research has ever properly tested whether family therapy works for these problems. That said, a lot of highly respected psychologists and psychiatrists swear by it, and just because no one has proved that it does work, does not mean to say that it doesn't. Family therapy may be a particularly good choice if you are worried about any of the relationships in your family. Family therapy takes many forms, and if you are invited to go along for family therapy, you can expect that both yourself, and partner if you have one, as well as all of your children, will be invited along. Sometimes other important family members (e.g. grandparents) will be invited along as well. The focus of family therapy is to subtly change the way family members interact with, and feel about, each other to produce a calmer and more harmonious family life. You may be surprised to find that you get not just one therapist, but several. Often, some of the therapists are not in the room with you but are watching behind a screen. They are there to observe and to give the main therapist extra advice on how they can help you.

Counselling

Again, we don't really know whether just getting 'counselling' is enough to help an anxious or depressed child. We simply haven't done the research to find out. If your child is offered counselling it is probably worth a try, but if things do not start to improve within a few weeks it may be worth seeking out alternative support.

Psychodynamic therapies

Again, no one has done any rigorous research to show whether psychodynamic therapy works for children or not. It has been tested a little bit on adults, but the evidence is shaky. Psychodynamic therapies can take many different forms, which I will not go in to here. However, many people now feel that these therapies are rather old fashioned and based on old theories, such as those put forward by Freud and Jung, rather than modern scientific theories of what is happening in the depressed or anxious mind. Traditional psychodynamic therapy has been a long-term therapy, with weekly sessions (or even more often) for anything up to several years. However, more recently, shorter forms of psychodynamic psychotherapy have been developed, which offer weekly sessions for six months or less. NICE have acknowledged that there is very little evidence for psychodynamic therapy being useful in treating depression, and so they have recommended that it be used as a last resort, if all other things have been tried. As with general counselling it may be worth giving this a go if you are offered it, but if you see no improvement within a few weeks, or if you or your child feel uncomfortable with the therapy, it may be worth seeking out alternative support.

Self help and support groups

As well as obtaining support from a professional, there is a lot that parents and carers can do to help themselves and their child. Some advice is given in this book. In addition, it can be invaluable to seek out the support of others who are in a similar position. The following groups give advice and support to sufferers of anxiety disorders:

National Phobics Society

The National Phobics Society is not, as it sounds, simply an organisation for sufferers of phobias, but is for anyone with any type of anxiety disorder. Their website has a plethora of information; they run therapy groups around the country (at the present time targeted mainly at adults) and can put you in touch with accredited therapists. Their website also has online support groups for various different anxiety problems.

Telephone: 0870 122 2325

Website: www.phobics-society.org.uk/

The Depression Alliance

The Depression Alliance is a UK-based charity for sufferers of depression. Their website contains lots of information about depression and they have details of local support groups for sufferers.

Telephone: 0845 123 23 20

Website: www.depressionalliance.org

Summary of Chapter Four

➡ If you think that your child is anxious or depressed, do go and get some help for them.

➡ Help is often available on the NHS, and if you take this route, you know that you will be getting a professional with some minimum basic qualifications.

➡ If you decide to get a therapist privately, be careful. Get a therapist from a reputable organisation and always ask them about their qualifications and experience.

➡ Many different sorts of therapy are available for treating anxiety and depression. However, the therapy with the most scientific evidence in its favour is Cognitive Behaviour Therapy (CBT).

5

Medications for anxious and depressed children

In an ideal world, giving medication to an anxious or depressed child would come only after other approaches (i.e. therapy) had been tried. Indeed, recent guidelines concur that this should be the case for both anxiety and depression (see below and chapter 4).

However, we do not live in an ideal world and sometimes waiting for therapy to become available would mean a long wait, so doctors choose to prescribe medication instead. Sometimes a child (or more rarely, and more worryingly, a parent) is reluctant to try therapy and would prefer to take medication.

In these instances, what choices are available, and what do you really need to know?

There are very many different medications that could be prescribed to your child and I would make you (and me) very bored if I listed them all. So, I will just talk about the most common medications that are prescribed for anxiety and depression. Some of the drugs are just intended for anxiety; others may be used to treat either anxiety or depression.

Drugs just for anxiety

Benzodiazepines

WHAT ARE THEY?

You may have heard of drugs such as Diazepam (Valium) or Lorazepam. These are a type of drug called 'benzodiazepines' and they are basically just sedatives. These are drugs that used to be prescribed to help people cope long-term with anxiety problems. This is not done any more because they have serious problems with addiction. You do occasionally meet people who have been on them for years. Very often these people want to stop taking them but cannot because of the serious withdrawal symptoms that they suffer. Because of this, these drugs are now prescribed only in very small, short doses. Usually GPs will only give them out to help people get through a very short period of stress.

CAN CHILDREN TAKE THEM?

Your child's GP or psychiatrist should be very reluctant indeed to prescribe one of these medications for your child or adolescent. In fact, just about the only time that youngsters are given these types of drugs nowadays is if they are having an operation; they are given a dose just before the surgery to make them feel calm and sleepy.

Beta blockers

These are a type of drug that were originally invented for use by heart patients. They work to make the heartbeat more regular. However, some heart patients who used beta blockers also reported that they felt less anxious when they used them. So, doctors started prescribing these drugs for people with certain anxiety problems, and for some patients they are very effective. It is thought that they help some cases of anxiety because, in making the heart beat more regularly, they reduce the palpitations that anxiety causes. For people where palpitations are a large part of their anxiety, beta blockers, therefore, can be effective. However, for most people just dealing with the palpitations is not enough and so beta blockers are not used so much these days; the newer medications are much better at dealing with the whole range of anxiety symptoms.

CAN CHILDREN TAKE THEM?

These drugs are sometimes prescribed for anxious children, but a doctor should have a very good reason for prescribing beta blockers rather than one of the newer medicines.

Drugs that work for both depression and anxiety

There are also lots of different sorts of these but the ones that are most often prescribed nowadays are called SSRIs, or Selective Serotonin Reuptake Inhibitors. They are called this because they work by altering the functioning of a natural chemical called 'serotonin' in the brain. There are also some even newer drugs called SNRIs, or Selective Noradrenaline Reuptake Inhibitors. These operate by altering another natural chemical known as 'noradrenaline' in the brain.

CAN CHILDREN TAKE THEM?

Although none of these SSRI and SNRI drugs are officially licensed for children or adolescents, they are often prescribed. The most common SSRIs and SNRIs are listed in Box 5.1, together with a note on whether they are recommended for children and adolescents. In general, even where a drug is sometimes prescribed for adolescents, there is very much more caution in prescribing it for younger children. This box also lists the names that the drugs are sometimes sold under.

Box 5.1. Common SSRI and SNRI medications for depression and anxiety

Drug Name	Sometimes sold as:	Recommended for under 18s?
Citalopram	Cipramil	Sometimes for anxiety Sometimes for depression[A]
Escitalopram	Cipralex	Sometimes for anxiety Not for depression
Paroxetine	Seroxat	Sometimes for anxiety Not for depression
Sertraline	Lustral	Sometimes for anxiety Sometimes for depression[A]
Fluvoxamine	Faverin	Sometimes for anxiety Not for depression
Fluoxetine	Prozac	Sometimes for anxiety Sometimes for depression[AB]
Venlefaxine	Efexor	Sometimes for anxiety Not for depression

[A] Endorsed for use in depression, but only in combination with psychological therapies. National Institute of Clinical Excellence Guidelines on Treatment of Depression in Children and Adolescents (2005).
[B] Endorsed for use by specialists for treating depression. Committee of Safety of Medicines (December 2003).

Until recently, most of these medications were widely prescribed for children and adolescents with anxiety and depression. However, in December 2003, a governmental body called the Committee for Safety of Medicines announced that, with the exception of Fluoxetine, these medications should be avoided by doctors treating depressed children and adolescents aged below 18, although they may be used with caution in children who are anxious but not depressed. This concern was raised because some research evidence was found suggesting that young people taking these medications had an increased number of thoughts about suicide. This decision was extremely controversial, with many doctors arguing that there was no evidence that children were actually more likely to go and harm themselves on these medications (even if they were perhaps having more thoughts of doing so). As a result of this controversy, more research is planned and it is possible that these drugs will one day be considered safe for young people. However, for now, doctors are told to use them only in very specific circumstances.

What are the circumstances in which doctors can prescribe medication for my child?

The NICE guidelines that I described in chapter 4 say that medications should not be prescribed for mild depression. For more severe depression, they should be prescribed only after psychological therapies have been tried, and that the psychological therapy should continue whilst the medication is being taken. For younger children aged 5–11 years, use of medication should be very cautious, even for severe depression where other approaches have failed. These guidelines suggest that fluoxetine should be tried first, and if that doesn't work or causes side effects, then Citalopram or Sertraline should be considered.

The National Institute for Clinical Excellence have not yet published guidelines for the treatment of anxiety in childhood. However, the British Association of Psychopharmacology recently published a report on the use of medications to treat anxiety. The report was not specifically concerned with the treatment of younger patients, but it concluded that the SSRIs should be used with caution in children and adolescents, and that, "it may be preferable to reserve pharmacological treatments for patients who do not respond to evidence-based psychological approaches."

What are the side effects of these medications?

All of these drugs have potential side effects, although most people do not get many, or only get them a little bit. The most common side effect for these SSRIs and SNRIs is feeling nauseous, and sometimes vomiting. Other gastro-intestinal symptoms are also quite common, as is change in appetite (it can go up or down) and headaches. These symptoms are generally not dangerous and subside after a few weeks, but they can feel pretty unpleasant while they last.

Other side effects are less common and depend on which medication is taken. Your child's doctor should run you through the important ones and any that you need to be worried about. When you get the medication, it is important to read the leaflet inside the pack. This will tell you about the side effects. It will also tell you how your child should take the medication and what to do if there is an overdose (accidental or otherwise).

What should I do when my child wants to come off medication?

You should always discuss your child coming off their medication with their doctor first. If your child has only been on the medication for a few weeks, the doctor will probably encourage them to stick with it a bit longer as it can take a few weeks to really get going.

Also, sometimes, when a child is doing well, it is tempting to take them off the medication as soon as possible. This should be the doctor's aim as well. However, we know from research that it is usually better to keep taking the medication for a while after you start feeling better (usually at least six months). This can help to stop the anxiety or depression from coming back again. However, this does have to be balanced with the need to keep the amount of medication that children take to the minimum, and your doctor should be happy to talk this decision through with you.

When the time comes to stop taking the medication, it is really important to do it gradually. Although the new medications (SSRIs and SNRIs) are not thought to be addictive (some people now argue that they are mildly addictive), stopping suddenly can cause nasty withdrawal reactions. Your doctor will advise you and your child how to cut down slowly.

Other things to note about medication

Sometimes people decide to go on medication instead of therapy because they think that it will be less hassle. However, this isn't always the case. Because of the worries about putting children on medication, the doctor will probably want to see your child very regularly – probably weekly at first, then once every couple of weeks. This will probably just be a short appointment to check that everything is OK, but it is important for your child's health and wellbeing that they make it along to these appointments. Also, with children especially, it sometimes takes a while to get the dose right. The doctor will want to start your child on the lowest dose possible and gradually increase this until the right level is reached. This process is called 'titration' and can take a few weeks (or even months) to get right.

A note on herbal remedies

There is much in the newspapers and magazines about herbal remedies for anxiety and depression. This is an exciting new area, but at the moment there is little evidence that these remedies work and that they are safe. So, I really think that you would be better off getting proper professional help for your child. There is a little bit of evidence that St John's Wort is helpful in some cases of depression in adults. However, as far as I am aware, it has not been studied in children. This makes me very worried. There are some rumblings that St John's Wort might have some occasional nasty side effects in adults, and I would be very concerned about giving it to a child or a teenager. It has not been studied and we simply do not know whether it is safe. I would urge you to talk to a doctor before you give your child any herbal remedies. If your child is given prescription drugs, such as those described in this chapter, you really *must* tell the doctor if they are also taking herbal remedies such as St John's Wort as these can interfere badly with the prescription drugs.

Summary of Chapter Five

➡ Although there is a role for using medication with some depressed and anxious children, psychological interventions should be tried first, where possible.

➡ A range of medications are available, but very few are recommended for use with children and adolescents.

➡ All medications can have some side effects, although for most people these are relatively minor.

➡ Your child should never stop taking their medication suddenly. Withdrawal should be done slowly, under the supervision of a doctor.

➡ It is very important that your child attends all their doctor's appointments when they are taking medication, so that their health can be closely monitored.

➡ Be very, very wary of giving your child herbal remedies.

SECTION TWO

In this second half of the book, I will talk about some things that you can do to help your child to overcome their difficulties.

The first six chapters in Section Two of this book are written in a very particular order. Psychologists have found from working with thousands of families that getting parents to introduce changes in this exact order is the best way to do it. Apart from anything else, if you try to do everything at once you will feel overwhelmed and will, without doubt, end up making mistakes and getting confused.

So, by all means read the book in one go, but when you come to start putting the advice into practice, start with chapter 6 and work through to chapter 11 in the right order.

Chapter 6 begins with some basic changes to diet, sleep and activity levels that can make all the difference to an anxious or depressed child. Chapter 7 talks about some simple changes to family life that can also really help. I would recommend that you read these two chapters and begin to put these things in place before you start tackling the suggestions that are made in the next chapters.

Chapter 8 talks about boosting your child's self-esteem and confidence. Try the tasks in this chapter for a couple of weeks before you start implementing chapter 9. Chapter 9 talks about using rewards to get more good and brave behaviour. Once you have got this going – and really find that your child is responding well to it – you and your child will be ready to go on to using the advice in chapter 10, which discusses how you can get rid of some of those annoying behaviours that make family life difficult. A word of warning, if you jump straight to chapter 10 (I know that the temptation is immense), it won't work. The tips in chapter 10 will really only work if you have the foundations from the earlier chapters in place. Once you have got the hang of the skills taught in the early part of Section Two, you should be finding that your child's emotional state is improving. However, by this point you should have the skills that you need to put in place the tips for dealing with worries and fears head on, as described in chapter 11.

Chapters 12 and 13 talk about special situations. Chapter 12 discusses what you can do if there is a serious family problem in the background. Chapter 13 talks about what schools can do to help an anxious or depressed child. These chapters are more stand-alone, and can be read and used at any point.

Finally, chapter 14 rounds off the book, and tells you what to expect of your depressed or anxious child in the future.

6

A few basics that can make
all the difference

In this chapter I will cover a few basic things that you as a parent can do to make a real difference to the way that your child is feeling.

Diet

We all know that what we eat can make a real difference to the way that we feel, and kids are no exception. Take a long, hard look at what your child eats and ask yourself whether this could be part of the problem.

Of course, it is impossible to have total control over what your child eats. However, you can have some impact on what they eat at home. Even if you just make sure that they eat a good breakfast, this will help.

I won't go on about what makes up a healthy diet as I'm sure that we are all well aware of how this should be. What I will do though, is talk about some of the diet problems that are particularly pertinent for anxious or depressed children.

Watch out for low blood sugar

You know that feeling when you are really hungry – tired, lethargic, can't cope with things, can't think straight? We all get it but if you are prone to anxiety or depression, this feeling feels ten times worse. This feeling happens when we have low blood sugar. So, it is a good idea to try to stop your child getting low blood sugar too often. Low blood sugar can happen for two reasons.

We get low blood sugar if we haven't eaten for several hours. So, you should try to make sure that your child eats regular meals, and has a healthy snack (e.g. fruit) between times, even if they do not feel very hungry. It is very important for these children to try to eat breakfast. If children skip breakfast, by the time they get to lunch they may not have eaten for 18 hours. No surprise that some children find school so difficult to cope with!

However, we can also get low blood sugar even if we have eaten in the last half-hour. This happens if we eat the wrong sorts of foods. If we eat something really sugary, this causes a spike in our blood sugar and we feel really good. But then our insulin kicks in and gobbles up all of the blood sugar, making it crash really low. Even though we may have eaten just half an hour ago, we will feel terrible. The foods that do this to our blood sugar are 'simple carbohydrates'. They are present in sweets, chocolate bars and fizzy drinks (but not low cal ones). Surprisingly, they are also present in some foods that we tend to think of as fairly healthy; for example, they are present in potatoes, white pasta and white bread. This is why after a big lunch of pasta or chips, we often feel really sleepy – the simple carbohydrates have made our blood sugar crash really low. Good alternatives are wholegrain foods, such as wholegrain cereals, wholegrain bread, and wholegrain pasta. These types of foods have really improved over the last few years and have thrown off their hippy reputation. You can get wholegrain bread and pasta that look and taste like the white versions – the kids won't even notice if you don't tell them.

I don't suggest that your child starts a strict regime of timetabled meals and snacks, and never eats a chocolate-bar or a potato again. However, it is worth cutting down on these foods, and making sure that, if your child has got to cope with something stressful today, they have had a good meal with not too many simple carbohydrates.

Caffeine

In sensitive individuals, drinking caffeine can trigger anxiety. Have you ever had that shaky feeling when you've drunk too much coffee? It can also make it difficult to get to sleep at night. Getting to sleep can be a difficult thing for anxious and depressed children, so it is best to cut down on their caffeine in the day and make sure that they stay well away from it for three hours before bedtime.

High levels of caffeine are present in coffee, both instant and ground coffee. It is also present in tea, although there is a little bit less here. It is also present in Cola drinks, including Diet Cola, and chocolate as well. So, all of these things need to be watched. If your child really doesn't want to give up tea/coffee/cola, then it is worth looking out for caffeine free versions – they are widely available now.

Sleep

Being over-tired can really make an anxious or depressed child feel worse. In fact, some people think that good quality sleep is the key to overcoming depression. So, it is really helpful if you can get your child into a routine of getting enough good quality sleep. Children vary in the amount of sleep that they need, so it is hard to give guidelines. The Sleep Foundation suggest that children aged 5 to 12 years need 9 to 11 hours sleep a night, and that teenagers need 8–1/2 to 9–1/2 hours. However, it isn't always this simple. For example, very often as children enter their teenage years, they need more sleep than when they were younger. In Box 6.1, I have given some pointers to working out whether your child is getting enough sleep.

Box 6.1. Is my child getting enough sleep?

Is it hard to get your child up in the morning?
Some people are slow wakers and can't just bounce out of bed, but if your child is still asleep ten minutes after you first try to wake him/her, they might not be getting enough sleep.
Does your child sometimes fall asleep during the day?
Does your child sleep for long periods at the weekend, as if they are catching up what they missed out on in the week?

If you answered Yes to any of these questions, it is possible that your child is not getting enough sleep. Remember that sometimes children need *more* sleep as they get older, and might need to go to bed earlier than younger brothers and sisters.

Box 6.2. Tips for Good Sleep

Try to have a good sleep routine for your child:

1. Have a wind-down period for an hour or so before bed. This should include relaxing activities, such as having a bath, watching some quiet TV, or reading.
2. Try to keep bedtime and waking-up time roughly the same time every day. This way, your child's body gets used to being sleepy at a certain time. This can be up to an hour later at weekends, but any later and your child's body starts to get confused.
3. Try to make your child's room quite quiet and dark. A little night-light is fine if they are afraid of the dark. However, if your child is a poor sleeper, do consider investing in some blackout curtains/blinds. These make

Continued

it much easier to get to sleep on light summer nights, and to stay asleep on light summer mornings.

4. This one tends to be a bit unpopular, but if sleep is a real problem for your child, don't let them go to sleep watching TV. Many kids have TVs in their rooms now, but falling asleep in front of the TV can increase the time that it takes to get to sleep, and can lead to disturbed sleep.

5. If you have an older child or teenager who finds it difficult to get to sleep, teach them the 'Alphabet Game'. The object of this game is to turn off the frantic mental activity that sometimes stops us getting to sleep. The rules of the game are that you go through the alphabet, and you have to think of an animal that starts with each letter. So, A for Ant, B for Bat, C for Cat, D for Dog ... etc. If you can't think of one (X is quite tricky ...) you just move on. It is important not to get tied up struggling to think of one, as this can get you too wound up to sleep. Once your child has got bored of doing this for animals, they can try it for other things, such as football teams, countries, girls' names, boys' names ... the list is endless.

Routines

Depressed and, in particular, anxious children benefit from having a (fairly) predictable routine. One of the problems for anxious and depressed kids is that they think that the world is unpredictable, and that horrible things can pop up out of the blue. Having a steady daily routine helps your child to be able to predict what is coming next and, therefore, to stay calm.

Having a routine means that your child always has a good idea of what is coming next. It also means that they can develop a bit of independence – so, for example, if they know that they always have breakfast and then go and get dressed, then they can learn to take themselves off after breakfast and get dressed, without waiting for someone to tell them what to do. This boosts children's confidence.

Having a routine does not mean that things are always exactly the same every day. That would not be good for children: they need to learn to cope with a little bit of change now and then. It just means having the same things happen at the same time, *most* of the time. If you are really not a 'routine' sort of family, then it is best to try to get a routine going just for the most stressful parts of the day: for most families, this is the morning, when everyone is trying to get up, dressed, fed and out at the same time.

Exercise

I'll let you into a secret, and I may be doing myself out of a job here! There has recently been some extremely interesting research into exercise and mental health. It has been shown that for mildly depressed and anxious people, taking up some gentle exercise is as good as having therapy! For people who are more troubled, exercise won't be a cure, but it will certainly help them on the road to recovery.

We all know that children these days don't do nearly as much exercise as we did when we were children. This is a shame – not just for their physical health, but for their mental health too. Take a good look at your child and tot up what exercise they do. Children and teenagers should really be doing a minimum of half an hour of really energetic activity every single day. In fact, in an ideal world, they would be doing a lot more.

If your child isn't coming close to doing half an hour of exercise a day, then it may be that they are being left with pent up energy, which is not doing their mental health any good. Not all kids are keen exercisers but if your child shows any interest in this area at all, do your very best to encourage them. Even reluctant children have some sorts of exercise that they find bearable. I, for instance, was a dreadfully unsporty child. I must confess that I even faked nose-bleeds to get out of hockey ... (sorry Miss

Lovatt, if you are reading), but my mum spotted that I didn't mind going swimming and arranged for me to go for swimming lessons so that I did at least get a bit of exercise. Likewise, even children who would shy away from a formal competitive activity will be happy to knock a ball around the garden for half an hour or bounce around their bedroom to some pop music.

'Pleasure and Mastery'

The final thing that I am going to talk about in this chapter is a technique that psychologists swear by. Depressed kids (and some anxious kids too) get worse if they sit around and dwell on things. They do much better if they get out and about and have some fun and do some things that make them feel pleased with themselves. Getting kids to do these things is called the 'Pleasure and Mastery' technique. It is called this because it gets kids doing things that make them feel 'pleasure' and things that give them a degree of 'mastery' – that is, things that make them feel pleased with themselves.

Although psychologists use this technique with children, it is parents who are ideally placed to get kids out and about and doing these things.

HOW TO DO IT

First of all, fill out the chart in Box 6.3 to see how much activity your child is doing at the moment. Your child should be aiming to do at least one interesting activity a day outside of school, not including watching TV. They should also be aiming to do something that is really energetic at least three times a week. If your child isn't doing this much, then increasing their activity should definitely help. Even if they are doing this bare minimum of activity, it will probably help to get them doing a bit more.

Box 6.3. Activity Chart

	Mon	Tue	Wed	Thu	Fri	Sat	Sun
7am–8am							
8am–9am							
9am–10am							
10am–11am							
11am–noon							
noon–1pm							
1pm–2pm							
2pm–3pm							
3pm–4pm							
4pm–5pm							
5pm–6pm							
6pm–7pm							
7pm–8pm							
8pm–9pm							
9pm–10pm							

Then, you and your child need to write a list of things that they enjoy doing in Box 6.5. In the case of a depressed child, this might feel like pulling teeth – depression makes you feel like you don't enjoy anything. As a parent, you know your child best and you are in an ideal position to gently remind your child of all of the things that they used to enjoy before the depression. We have left a space for you and your child to write down their list. In case you are struggling for ideas, Box 6.4 lists some things that lots of kids like doing, to get you started.

Once you have drawn up a list, fill in the activity sheet in Box 6.3 or one of the spare copies at the back of this book. The aim is to build up your child's activity levels. At first, you need to go easy – don't overwhelm your child. Try just to fill in an extra hour or so a day. Fill in the form jointly with your child and whilst being encouraging, and mildly pushy, do not ask too much of them to start with. Over the coming weeks you can gradually build up the amount of activities that your child is engaging in.

Box 6.4. Activities that kids often enjoy doing

- Having a friend round to visit
- Going to visit friends
- Collecting something
- Going to clubs, e.g. scouts, brownies
- Going to social events, e.g. disco's
- Going to a child-friendly place to eat
- Going swimming / skating / skateboarding
- Playing pop music far too loud
- Going to the cinema with a friend
- Making something – e.g. a model or a painting
- Working on a skill, e.g. dancing class, horse riding, musical instrument

Box 6.5. Activities that my child enjoys (or used to enjoy)

1. ... ...
2. ... ...
3. ... ...
4. ... ...
5. ... ...
6. ... ...
7. ... ...
8. ... ...
9. ... ...
10. ... ...

HOW TO GET YOUR KIDS TO DO ALL OF THESE THINGS

Of course, all of these things are much easier said than done. Getting an anxious, and particularly a depressed, child to engage in new activities is pretty hard work. If you struggle with this, chapter 9 of this book gives lots of tips for getting kids to do what you want them to do with the minimum of arguments.

Summary of Chapter Six

- Our mental state is strongly affected by our life-style. In particular, you can really help by making sure that your child:

  ➡ Has a reasonably healthy diet, with regular meals and snacks

  ➡ Isn't taking in too much caffeine

  ➡ Gets enough sleep

  ➡ Has a reasonably consistent routine

  ➡ Does a bit of exercise

  ➡ Is keeping busy with fun and interesting activities

7

A stable, safe, predictable(ish) home life

The Seven Confident Thoughts

When parents come to our groups for families whose children are anxious or unhappy, we always have a huge poster on the wall. It is entitled 'The Seven Confident Thoughts'. The Seven Confident Thoughts are printed in Box 7.1.

These are the Seven Thoughts of happy, confident kids. These seven thoughts are the building blocks of confidence. If you can get your child to think these seven thoughts, then you have won the battle!

Box 7.1. The Seven Confident Thoughts

- The world is a pretty safe place
- I can cope with most things
- Bad things don't usually happen to me
- Bad things don't pop up out of the blue
- I have some control over the things that happen to me
- People are pretty nice really
- Other people respect me

Take another look at 'The Seven Confident Thoughts'. Children who think in this way will be confident and outgoing and will be ready to cope with the problems that life throws at them. So, how can you make your kids think these thoughts? Parents always ask me this. Usually with a look of panic on their faces. "You are the therapist!" they say. "We don't know how to change someone's thoughts!"

But making someone think certain thoughts is not magic. In fact, parents are absolutely brilliant at it. Think about other thoughts that your child has. Which football team does your child think is the best in the world? I'll bet it's the same as Mum's or Dad's. Did your child ever wait for Father Christmas or the Tooth Fairy? And who put that idea into their heads? That's right, parents are brilliant at shaping the way that their children think about things, and parents are in the perfect position to give their children 'The Seven Confident Thoughts'.

Sometimes, we can get children to believe things just by telling them. Sometimes we have to be a bit cleverer than that. To get your child to believe 'The Seven Confident Thoughts', you will have to put in a bit of effort. But don't worry, in this chapter and those that follow I will explain just how you can do this.

Step One – Special Time

Giving your child ten minutes of your undivided
attention every day

The first thing that you can do to give your child the Seven Confident Thoughts involves spending a bit of extra time with your child. We call this 'Special Time'. For an anxious or depressed child, you will need to spend about ten minutes every day doing this. During Special Time, you need to follow some simple rules, outlined in Box 7.2.

Obviously, a teenager is not going to want to sit down and play snap with you, like a younger child might. However, a sit-down

Box 7.2. Special Time

- Try to do Special Time every day.
- Ask your child what they want to do for the 10 minutes. Let them choose anything, within reason.
- During the 10 minutes, give the child your undivided attention. Turn the TV off, ignore the phone, don't try to do anything else (e.g. cook the dinner, do the ironing) at the same time.
- Have a nice time with your child. Use this time to give your child lots of praise.
- Give your child lots of affection during these 10 minutes – give them hugs and kisses if they like that. If they don't like hugs and kisses, at least try to show some physical affection – put an arm round their shoulder, or touch them on the arm a few times.
- Let the child be in charge during these 10 minutes. If they want to change the rules of the game that you are playing, that is fine. If they act silly or show off, let it pass. During these 10 minutes, it is all about having a relaxed time. Don't criticise your child unless they actually do something dangerous.
- Don't use this time to teach your child – there are plenty of other times for learning. These 10 minutes are just about enjoying your time together.
- Try not to ask too many questions during these 10 minutes. Asking questions stops your child's mind from relaxing and going with the flow. Questions are fine at any other time, but not in this special 10 minutes.

with a cup of tea, for a bit of a gossip, will be just as good. Having your undivided attention and warmth for ten minutes works wonders for older kids too.

Quiz: 10 minutes Special Time

Which of the Seven Confident Thoughts do you think that the ten minutes Special Time helps to boost for your child? Tick the ones that you think:

1. The world is a pretty safe place.
2. I can cope with most things.
3. Bad things don't usually happen to me.
4. Bad things don't pop up out of the blue.
5. I have some control over the things that happen to me.
6. People are pretty nice really.
7. Other people respect me.

Answer: You could argue that this special time works on all seven of the Confident Thoughts. However, I think it works most strongly for: 1. "The world is a pretty safe place" (during this Special Time, your child should feel warm and safe and relaxed); 5. "I have some control over the things that happen to me" (during this special time, your child is in control of what happens – a rare event for most children); 6. "People are pretty nice really" (you did remember to be nice, didn't you?); 7. "Other people respect me" (you have been showing your child that you respect them).

Step Two – Happy Family Times

Ask yourself this question: when was the last time you did something nice together as a family? If it was more than a week ago then you owe it to yourselves as a family to give more attention to having nice times together.

Try to have at least one Happy Family Time every week. These times don't have to be expensive or take up too much time. Try to pick something that has appeal for all of you. Here are some ideas for Happy Family Times:

- Take a picnic to the park
- Play a game of cards together
- Play a board game together
- Make something together – a cake, a painting

- A trip to a museum or art gallery – most of them are free nowadays
- Or, ask your child what they would like to do ... and try to be open-minded ...

Step Three – Communicating well within your family

Communicating well is really important in any family. But for a family with an anxious or depressed child, it is extra important.

COMMUNICATING NASTY SURPRISES

Mark, who was eight years old, was really scared of the dentist. No one really knew why he was scared of the dentist because he had never had a bad experience going to the dentist. However, his mum was also scared of the dentist and thinks that Mark might have learnt to be scared by hearing her talking about how scared *she* was. Anyway, whenever it was time to go the dentist, his mum put off telling Mark for as long as possible. She knew he would get really upset and make a fuss. So, instead, she waited to the last minute before she told him. Usually she only told him on the morning that they were due to go. This always caused the most enormous tantrums and upset, but Mum figured that one morning of this was better than a whole week. What do you think?

Was Mark's mum doing the right thing in not telling him until the last minute? I asked this question to a group of parents who were coming along to our parents' course. At the start of the course, they all said, "yes," she was doing the right thing – she was keeping the amount of time that he was upset down to a bare minimum – she was a kind parent. Then I asked them again at the end of the course, and every single one of them gave a new answer. They all said that, "no," Mark's mum should have given him a couple of days warning before they had to go to the dentist. When I asked them why they had changed their minds, one very smart mum, called Mel, pointed to our poster of the Seven Confident Thoughts and said "Mark needs to learn that bad things don't usually pop up out of the blue. If he is going to get over his anxiety, he needs to know that nasty surprises are not just around the corner." All of the parents agreed with Mel, and so did I.

These parents are right. If we think that nasty surprises can just jump out and bite us, we are going to be on edge all of the time. However, if we know that we usually get a bit of warning so that we can prepare ourselves for something scary, then we can afford to relax a little bit.

So, how much warning should we give to a child? This is a tricky question, and depends on how old your child is. As a rule of thumb, I would say the following:

- For a small child, up to about four years of age – they only need a couple of hours of warning; they don't have a very good understanding of time and any more warning than a couple of hours will feel like weeks away.
- With an older child, say five to seven years of age – I would try to give a day or two of warning.
- With a child aged eight to eleven – I would give several days to a week of warning.
- With children older than eleven – give them as much warning as you can; they have a right to know if something nasty is coming up and, if they find out that you have been keeping a secret from them, they may lose some of their trust in your honesty.

Good co-parenting

Co-parenting is how parents work together to bring up their children. In recent years, we have begun to understand how important good co-parenting is to the welfare of children. Even if you are bringing up your child on your own, you should read this section. You may have the main responsibility for your child but there are usually others – grandparents, childminders, and so on – who have a role, and it is really important to make sure that you all work together.

Do children need consistency? In short, yes they do. The very best parenting is when all those who care for a child work to the same rules. If a child has very different rules from Mum and Dad, and then different rules again from Gran, they can get confused and scared. It is much easier to feel confident if you are very clear about what the rules are, and what will happen if you break them!

However, let's be realistic here: I've never met a family where all of the adults have the same rules for the children. It is completely normal and healthy for people to have different ideas about how children should be raised, and usually one parent is a bit more lenient than the other. So, what do you do if you have different views to the other important people in your child's life?

DISCUSS, DISCUSS, DISCUSS

The first thing to do is to discuss what rules you want for your children. If you know what other people think, it is so much easier to fit in with them. I will talk more about deciding rules and punishments later, but for an anxious or depressed child it is best to have just a small number of very clear rules. If the other person does not agree with your rule, then explain gently, and with a smile, what your reasoning is. Then listen to their response, and give it some real thought.

COMPROMISE, COMPROMISE, COMPROMISE

Life is all about making little compromises, and if your children see adults settling their differences nicely by making compromises, this is an excellent lesson for them. Very few rules are so important that they can't be altered a little bit.

I'll let you into a little secret. Psychologists who work on dispute resolution love compromise. They have shown, through lots of research, that if you give a little compromise to your opponent, they are quite likely to respond by giving you a big compromise in return! So if you want to get someone to see your point of view, give a little ground on something else.

So, what if you do disagree with the other parent/gran/child-minder on something? Sometimes we just have to accept the fact that another person is stuck in their ways, and we are not going to change them. Look at the case of Joe below.

Joe's parents were divorced. They had tried really hard to keep the separation amicable, and they were both deter-mined, for Joe's sake, to keep being the best parents pos-sible. However, human nature intervened and Joe's parents started each doing things their own way. Joe's mum liked Joe to have a bath each night and to go to bed at 8.30, so when Joe stayed with her, that is what happened. Joe's dad was more laid back about these things. He didn't make Joe have a bath every night, and let him stay up until 9.30 or 10pm. Joe's mum got upset about this as she thought that Joe would get tired, and she was worried about him being a bit grubby. Of course, you can guess what happened. When he was at Mum's house, Joe complained about having a bath and having to go to bed early. Mum, understandably, got upset about this and every time it happened she got more and more annoyed. In the end, she became very fed up and just told Joe that she thought his dad was being irresponsible.

Do you think that Joe's mum did the right thing? Well, I think that we can all put ourselves in her shoes and see why she was annoyed. However, by undermining his dad, she was really not doing Joe any favours. Kids really need to trust their parents, and need to believe that their parents are pretty good at parenting. If Joe begins to think that his dad is not a good dad, then this can really feed into his insecur-ities. Also, kids can be relied upon to go and report what was said to the other parent. Hearing that your ex-wife thinks that you are an incompetent parent is not nice and is not going to do much to foster a good co-parenting relationship.

In summary, it is best for all of the adults in a child's life to have consistent rules.

If rules are a bit different, this is OK. However, if this is the case, all of the adults must work very hard to give the child the picture that they are all working together, and that although they have different rules, they respect each others' decisions.

As a good start to your co-parenting relationship, why not get your child's other parent (or any parent figures) to read this book. The skills taught in this book work much better if everyone around the child is doing them.

Also, if you are taking your child along to see a professional for help with their depression or anxiety, try to get other important family members to come too. Very often the therapist will have advice for the family, and this works much better if everyone takes it on board.

Summary of Chapter Seven

- In this chapter, the need for a safe and predictable(ish) home life is discussed.

  ➡ The *Seven Confident Thoughts* are introduced. These are the building blocks of a confident, happy child. Creating a safe, predictable environment for your child is the first step in developing the 'Seven Confident Thoughts'.

  ➡ *Special Time*, preferably one-to-one, with your child, is very important in building the 'Seven Confident Thoughts'. Ten minutes every day, following a few simple rules, can really move your child onwards.

  ➡ *Happy Family Times*. Every family needs times when they are just together enjoying themselves, rather than rushing round, doing all of the things that busy families have to do. These times are particularly important for an anxious or depressed child.

➡ *Family Communication*. It is important to have open and clear lines of communication between the adults in the family, and between the adults and the children. It is best if all of the adults set the same rules for the child. With good communication and consistency between parents, anxious and depressed children can build up their 'Seven Confident Thoughts'.

8

Boosting your child's self-esteem and confidence

Remember in chapter 7, I introduced the concept of the Seven Confident Thoughts? Here they are again in Box 8.1:

Box 8.1. The Seven Confident Thoughts

- The world is a pretty safe place
- I can cope with most things
- Bad things don't usually happen to me
- Bad things don't pop up out of the blue
- I have some control over the things that happen to me
- People are pretty nice really
- Other people respect me

We have already thought about how you can use time with your child to boost these thoughts, and in chapters 9 and 10, we will see how you can manage your child's difficult behaviour in the right way to ensure that they grow up thinking in this way.

In this chapter, we will look at some extra things that you can do to boost the Seven Confident Thoughts, and with them, your child's confidence and self esteem.

Play to your child's strengths

Everyone has things that they seem to do well at. Things that just seem to come a bit more easily than others. What are your child's strengths? When I say strengths, I'm not talking about things that your child is brilliant at. You don't have to have an Olympic medal or a PhD in something for it to be one of your strengths. It just has to be something that you like doing and have a bit of a knack for.

In the space below, write down some things that your child seems to do better at. Some examples to start you off are shown in Box 8.2:

Box 8.2. Examples of strengths

- School subjects – e.g. maths, science, English, languages, art, P.E., cookery, metalwork
- Sports – e.g. football, swimming, rounders, netball, dancing, ice skating
- Crafts – e.g. painting, drawing, designing cards, making things
- Personality traits – kindness, good listener, good with little children, good with older people, good organiser or leader, good team member
- Others – playing guitar / piano / drums, dressing well

In Box 8.3, write down your own child's strengths. Think of as many as you can.

Box 8.3. Things that my child is good at

……………………………………………………………………………………
……………………………………………………………………………………
……………………………………………………………………………………
……………………………………………………………………………………
……………………………………………………………………………………
……………………………………………………………………………………

I hope that you managed to think of quite a few things to put in the box. If we want good self-esteem, then we all need things that we are good at. If you couldn't think of many things, then this is likely to be a big part of your child's difficulties. So, what do you do if you couldn't think of many things? The first step is to try to find out if there is anything that you may have missed. Ask friends, family, teachers, whether there is anything that you have missed: some little special qualities that may have passed *you* by might have been noticed by other people.

When you have identified these things that your child is good at, the next step is to use them to boost your child's confidence. This is easier to do than it sounds. However, because your child is suffering from anxiety or depression, this will need a bit of extra effort on your part.

SO WHAT DO I HAVE TO DO?

It's easy. You need to take a good long look at the list of good qualities that you have drawn up for your child, and then every time you see your child doing one of the things on the list – praise, praise, praise! Your objective is to let your child know how proud of them you are, and to let them know that they have qualities that are really appreciated.

I want to set you a challenge for the next twenty-four hours. I would like you to try to praise your child, *at least five times*, for some of the qualities on the list. You can also praise them for other things, of course, including things that they are not good at but have tried hard at. However, it is important that children learn about their own strengths, and they will do this every time that you praise them for one.

Take another look at the Seven Confident Thoughts in Box 8.1. Which of the thoughts do you think this technique is working on? As with most of the techniques in this book, this is shaping up all of the seven thoughts, but in particular, I think that it is working on: *I can cope with most things. People are pretty nice really. Other people respect me.*

Remember to keep praising your child, not just for things that they need a bit of a boost on (things that they are scared of, or are in the process of learning) but on things that they are naturally quite good at too.

Push them to try new things

When we get anxious or depressed, one of the first things that we do is retreat into our shell. We stop trying new things and we even stop doing a lot of our old things. This is a real problem. Kids who are anxious or depressed already think pretty badly of themselves. They think that they can't cope with things, that no one respects them, that life is too hard and no fun. We need to turn these thoughts round, so that they are thinking more in line with the Seven Confident Thoughts. One way to turn it around is to get kids pushing themselves a bit. Get them testing out how it feels to do new things (it generally feels great) and get them proving to themselves that they are capable of doing amazing things when they try.

So, get your kids going on some new and exciting activities. Box 8.4 has some suggestions, but you know your child best, so do add in things that you think will work for them.

Of course, getting a reluctant child to take up a new activity is easier said than done. But fear not, the next two chapters will focus on techniques that maximise your power as a parent, to get your kid to do things they don't really want to do!

Making sure your child gets a confidence boost every week

By now you should have a list of the things that your child is good at and have some ideas for new activities that they could

Box 8.4. New activities for your child to try

> A new sport – e.g. football, netball, swimming, dancing, martial arts
> A new hobby – making cards, baking, collecting postcards / stamps etc.
> A new club – e.g. guides, cubs, brownies, scouts, youth club, drama club
> Add some of your own ideas here:
>
> ... ...
> ... ...
> ... ...
> ... ...
> ... ...
> ... ...
> ... ...
> ... ...
> ... ...
> ... ...
> ... ...
> ... ...
> ... ...
> ... ...
> ... ...
> ... ...
> ... ...
> ... ...
> ... ...
> ... ...
> ... ...
> ... ...
> ... ...
> ... ...
> ... ...
> ... ...

try out. Go back to your activity sheets that we talked about in chapter 6 and put some of these activities into your child's activity plan for the next week.

Summary of Chapter Eight

- This chapter gives tips on how to raise your child's self esteem and confidence.

  ➡ Have a good think about things that your child has a strength in. This can be schoolwork, a hobby, sport, or even a personal quality. Then make sure you praise this strength at every opportunity.

  ➡ Encourage your child to try new things. Finding new things that we enjoy gives anyone a boost, and learning that we can do something that looks hard is a real boost to the self esteem.

  ➡ Go back to chapter 6 and your child's activity sheets and put in some of the new activities and some activities that your child has strength in. This way, they will be having really powerful confidence boosting experiences every single week.

9

On their best behaviour: getting your kids to do what you want without tears and tantrums

Part 1: Getting more good behaviour

One of the biggest mistakes that parents of depressed or anxious children can make is the way in which they set and enforce rules. Most parents either go too strict and risk increasing the stress on their child, or back off from their child so much that they can almost get away with murder. Both situations are bad for anxious/depressed kids. Have a look at the cases below and on page 77.

 Kyle was ten years of age. He was referred to a clinical psychologist because of depression and behaviour problems. His parents reported that he just sulked all day, went for long periods without talking, and repeatedly ran out of school during the day. He also had lots of tantrums and could be really aggressive with other children. The psychologist, James, did an assessment of Kyle's home life. James discovered that Kyle's family were very, very strict. There were hundreds and hundreds of rules about what he should and should not do. For instance, one day, when the family came for an appointment,

Continued

James saw Kyle's dad yelling at Kyle because he was walking down the hospital drive rather than on the grass at the side. James asked Kyle about this later, and Kyle said that he hadn't really known where to walk because the grass was muddy, and there wasn't a proper path, so he walked at the side of the (very quiet) drive instead. Kyle knew that if he walked on the grass and got muddy, he would get shouted at. Sometimes, however, there were so many rules that Kyle didn't even know that they existed. His dad told him off because he was slouching in his chair and Kyle started crying. He told James that he didn't know that he was supposed to sit up straight when he visited the psychologist. Kyle's family used lots of punishments to try to get him to behave how they wanted. He was often grounded for weeks at a time; his parents smacked him lots and, one time, his dad confiscated a sticker which he had earned from his teacher, because he did not hang up his coat when he came home.

James worked hard with Kyle's family. Although he didn't think that they had caused Kyle's problems, he did think that their extreme strictness was stopping Kyle from developing into a confident, mature, young man. James was keen to instil 'The Seven Confident Thoughts' into Kyle, but he was worried that Kyle's parents' strictness was hindering this.

Looking at Kyle's story above, which of the Seven Confident Thoughts do you think that Kyle's parents might need to work on? The Seven Confident Thoughts are reproduced again in Box 9.1, below.

Box 9.1. The Seven Confident Thoughts

- The world is a pretty safe place
- I can cope with most things
- Bad things don't usually happen to me
- Bad things don't pop up out of the blue
- I have some control over the things that happen to me
- People are pretty nice really
- Other people respect me

Lauren was eleven years old when she was referred to the hospital for help with her anxiety. She was often tearful, especially if someone told her that she had done something wrong. She was very nervous of new situations, and had started refusing to go to school on some mornings.

Her parents were at the end of their tether. They desperately didn't want to see her upset so they had learnt not to make any demands on her at all. So, although Lauren was starting to get tired by about 9 pm, her parents didn't dare to tell her to go to bed. Instead they let her stay up until they went to bed at about 11 pm. If she wanted to sleep in their bed, they let her. If she was upset when she woke up in the morning, they knew that she would have a tantrum if they tried to make her go to school, so they let her stay off and Mum would have to take a day off work to stay with her.

Lauren's parents were trying to be nice, but her psychiatrist, Fiona, thought that their niceness was actually making things worse. In letting Lauren do what she wanted all of the time, her parents weren't giving her any boundaries. Children need a routine and they need to know what the house rules are. If there are no rules then they can start to feel very out of control, which can lead to anxiety. As well as this, Lauren was constantly exhausted. She was also being allowed to avoid the things that she felt scared of (e.g. school) which, as we shall see in chapter 11, is very bad for anxiety.

The psychiatrist, Fiona, helped Lauren's mum and dad to decide on a few house rules (e.g. bedtime, rules about going to school every day) and gave them some tips for enforcing these rules in a calm and consistent way. Over the course of the next few months Lauren seemed to become happier and more confident. Her parents were more able to put their foot down without fear of tantrums and the household ran more smoothly.

Well, if you said "all of them", then James the psychologist agrees with you. He thought that Kyle had little chance of developing any of the confident thoughts with his parents being so strict. Kyle's parents were invited onto a parenting course where they learnt to have fewer rules, and to enforce them in much gentler ways. By the end of the course, Kyle's behaviour was much, much better. He had far less tantrums, he seemed happier and was more talkative. His teacher said that he was doing much better at school and had started getting on better with the other children. As a surprise bonus, Kyle's dad reported that Kyle had started doing as he was told the first time that he was asked. As a result, dad felt much more relaxed and was hardly smacking and shouting at all. Everyone Wins!

So how do you enforce house rules for these sorts of kids?

As Kyle's parents found, shouting and making threats (a) didn't work, and (b) made Kyle's behaviour and his depression worse. So, their psychologist, James, taught them some completely different techniques. When he told Kyle's parents what he wanted them to do, they were not impressed at first (James thinks there might even have been a snort from Kyle's dad ...). So what exactly did he ask them to do?

Praise

James asked Kyle's mum and dad to make a list of good behaviours that they wanted to see more of in Kyle. Try doing this yourself in Box 9.2 below.

Box 9.2. What behaviours do you want to see more of?

> Write a list of things that you want to see more of in your child. Try to include good behaviours, e.g. tidying the table after dinner, doing homework without being nagged, coming in on time; and also confident behaviours, e.g. going to school with a smile on their face, joining in more activities at school.
>
> 1. ... ...
> 2. ... ...
> 3. ... ...
> 4. ... ...
> 5. ... ...
> 6. ... ...

Parents often find this a really hard thing to do. As humans we are programmed to think of the negative things that we want to see less of – for example, less crying, less arguing with your sister, less tantrums. Kyle's parents fell into this trap. At first, their list looked like this:

1. Less crying on the way to school
2. Getting told off less for fighting at school
3. Less answering back when you are told to do something

James was worried about this. He explained to the parents that this list would mean that they would be on the look out for bad behaviour in Kyle. With this negative frame of mind it was no wonder that they were shouting so much and that Kyle felt negative about himself. James explained that he wanted everyone to learn a much more positive mindset. So, together, James and Kyle's parents rewrote the list. Afterwards, it looked like this:

1. More smiling on the way to school
2. More happy reports from the teacher at the end of each day
3. More doing as you are asked first time

James asked Kyle's mum and dad to make a really big effort to look out for these behaviours. Whenever they spotted these behaviours they were to give Kyle lots of praise and attention. Kyle's parents agreed (Dad was more reluctant than Mum, but nonetheless, he decided to give it a go). James gave Kyle's parents some tips on praising. These are in Box 9.3.

I have made all of this sound really easy. But I do appreciate that in fact, learning to enforce rules using praise instead of shouting is really hard. To make parents at our clinic feel more at ease with the new techniques, and so that they know they are not alone when they find it hard, we invented some agony-aunt columns, where fictitious parents write in with their struggles. Her advice can befound in Box 9.5 on page 81.

Box 9.3. Tips on getting the most out of praise

- Give it whenever you see a behaviour you like – e.g. a good behaviour, or a brave behaviour
- Sound really positive when giving praise
- Don't follow praise with a criticism (e.g. "Well done for finally tidying your room, why can't you do that every day?")
- Make it really clear what you are giving the praise for (e.g. "Well done for getting on well with your sister at granny's today, I was really proud of you!")
- Give praise straight away after the behaviour you liked; if you leave it too long, it won't work as well

Box 9.4. Some examples of praise to get you started

- "You are putting your toys away really nicely!"
- "Good boy for doing as you were asked first time!"
- "Thank you for coming in on time!"
- "I really like it when you share your toys with Sam!"
- "Well done for going into town on your own!"
- "I'm very pleased with you for trying some cabbage!"
- "Well done for going upstairs in the dark!"
- "Wow, what a wonderful job you've done on your home-work!"
- "You're such a big girl for stroking that dog!"
- "Well done for being brave and going to Amy's party!"
- "I'm really proud of you for going to school today!"

Rewards and bribes

Another really fantastic way of getting kids to do what you want, when you want, is to use rewards. Lots of parents are a bit dubious when we tell them this. They feel as if this is bribing their child for good behaviour, when they should just be good without having to have a treat. However, when parents ask us this we always say to them, "Would you go to work if some-one didn't pay you to?" I know I wouldn't (and I really like

Box 9.5. Dr Drusilla answers parents' questions about praising their children

"Dear Dr Drusilla,

My child should be able to go to the toilet on his own by his age. Should I really be praising him just because he can now go with me standing outside the door?"

Agatha Arkwright, Timbuktu

Dr Drusilla says:

"Dear Agatha,

Going to the loo alone might seem easy to you, but to your child, it is as scary as jumping off a mountain. If your child has had to pluck up courage to do this, then you should definitely give him lots of attention for this. Praise and rewards are the best form of attention that you can give a child. If he gets clear praise for going to the loo with you just outside the door, perhaps next time he will feel more brave, and be able to tinkle with you a little bit further away. Hang in there, Agatha!"

"Dear Dr Drusilla,

My child has been so naughty today. Honestly, sometimes I think I should have called him 'Damien'. I know I should praise him when he is good, but today, when he tidied up the table after dinner, I was just too angry to praise him. What is a girl to do?"

Tabitha Titchmarsh, Outer Mongolia

Dr Drusilla says:

"Dear Tabitha,

I know how you feel. They really can be little monkeys. But trust me! Kids are smart, if he starts getting more attention for the good stuff, then he will switch his energies to being good. With a bit of luck, he will soon be putting so much effort into getting attention for being good, that he won't have any energy left for being naughty!"

my job). Most of the time, we only do things that are a chore, or that feel a bit scary, because there is something in it for us. "Aha," I hear you say, "But what about all the times when we do things for nothing – when we help out a friend for no reward, or give something to charity?" It's true, on those occasions, we are not getting anything concrete back, but most of us really enjoy that warm glow that we get when we do something nice or kind. Unfortunately, psychologists don't think that this 'warm glow' is naturally built-in with kids. It is something that they have to learn. And we know from studying children, that the ones who turn out the kindest and most charitable are those who have learnt that doing something good gets them praise and the occasional little treat. In other words, children need to learn that being good feels good. They do this by having lots of chances to do well and getting rewarded for it. Sadly, for depressed children, and for some anxious kids too, feeling good doesn't come easily, so parents have to work extra hard to teach them that doing good things really does feel good. They can do this by working hard at giving rewards for the behaviour that they want to see in their children.

So, how do you use rewards to get the best out of your anxious or depressed child?

There are some tricks to getting rewards to work as well as possible, especially if your child is depressed or lacking in confidence.

Give rewards for behaviour that you want to see more of

- Give them for good behaviour
- Give them for brave and confident behaviour

You can use rewards to encourage any behaviour at all. This can be a good behaviour (e.g. doing your homework) or a brave behaviour (e.g. going to the toilet on your own).

Give the reward as soon as possible after the good or brave behaviour

This is especially important for younger children. If you leave the reward too long, your child might have forgotten what the reward is for, and it will lose its power.

Get the behaviour before you give the reward

If you give the reward before you get the behaviour, what will happen? That's right, your child might well pocket the reward, and then refuse to do what you wanted anyway! Always give the reward after you have got the behaviour that you wanted; that way, if you don't get the behaviour, you can hang on to the reward.

Stick to your promises

If you promise to give a reward later (e.g. "because you went to school today, we will go to the cinema on Saturday"), you must stick to your promise, even if the child behaves badly later. Lots of parents get this wrong and end up losing their child's trust. See page 84 for a case where just this happened.

Box 9.6. Summary of how to use rewards to get the behaviour you want

- Give Rewards for behaviours that you want to see more of
- Give the reward as soon as possible after the good or brave behaviour
- Get the behaviour before you give the reward
- Stick to your promises
- Make the reward the right size for the behaviour
- Give lots of clear praise at the same time as the reward
- Choose the reward wisely
- Use Ready-Made Rewards

Michael was 13 years old and referred to the hospital because of depression. His depression made him very grumpy and he frequently had outbursts at home and school. Michael's mum was working on an activity programme to get Michael out and about and enjoy himself more – the depression had meant that he had given up all of his favourite activities (see chapter 6). Michael's mum had, after much haggling, persuaded Michael to go to scouts one evening. He really didn't want to go but she said that if he went, she would let him stay up a bit late that night to watch a big football match on TV. Michael agreed and went to scouts, and actually had quite a nice time. However, when he came back he was very tired and was tetchy with his mum. His mum got really fed up with him (raising a depressed child is very hard work, as you know) and couldn't face having him up late. So, she told him off and sent him to bed early.

The next day she really wanted Michael to go swimming with his friends after school because she knew that he would actually enjoy it when he got there and that it would be good for him. Michael, of course, thought differently and didn't want to go. So, his mum offered a reward. She said, "After you have gone swimming, we will go to the Chinese take-away for tea." She knew this was a big treat for Michael. But to her surprise he said "NO!" Nothing she could say would change his mind. When he came to the hospital for his next appointment, Michael's mum complained that the rewards were just not working. I could guess why, but I wanted Mum to guess for herself. She had no idea but before I could have a chance to explain, Michael piped up – "Yeah, but when you say I can have a treat, I don't believe you. You'll just get in a bad mood and change your mind, like you did after scouts. It's a waste of time, cos I won't get the reward even if I've done what you wanted. I just don't trust you!"

The moral of the tale is always, *always* give a reward if you have promised it, no matter how vile your child is later on. If they have kept their side of the bargain, then you need to keep yours too. Otherwise, they will just stop trusting you.

Give lots of clear praise with the reward

If you are giving a reward, you are doing it so that your child will learn to associate their good behaviour with feeling nice. If they don't know what behaviour they are being rewarded for, this won't work, so you need to tell them.

Choose the reward carefully

Always choose a reward because your child will like it, not because you will like it! I once worked with a lovely family who did very well with their anxious six year old. However, they complained that rewards just didn't seem to work very well. The main reward that Mum chose to use was letting her little boy stay up half an hour extra at night. I couldn't think what the problem was until the little boy himself pointed out that during this half hour, the entire family sat down to watch Coronation Street. Whilst the rest of the family were total Corrie addicts, which meant that this was a lovely treat for them at the end of a busy day, the little boy just didn't get it at all. He just sat there, bored and miserable, and didn't see it as a reward worth working for. When we thought up some rewards that he did like (mostly involving time on the PlayStation) then suddenly the rewards started working like magic.

Ready-made rewards

If you are going to give your child a treat anyway, e.g. going to the park, tell them it is because they did something good. For example, "I was so proud of you for going to the dentist, so now I am taking you to the park." I know some families who have got so good at using this trick that their children feel as if they are getting ten treats a day! This is fantastic for everyone. The parents don't have to keep coming up with new ideas and extra time and money for treats, and the children feel as if they are really liked, respected and valued. What is more, their good behaviour and their confident behaviour comes on brilliantly.

The reward doesn't need to be big

Rewards do not need to be big. Most of us are not millionaires. We cannot afford to buy our child a bike every time they have tidied up their room or done their homework. Rewards come in all shapes and sizes and some of the best ones are absolutely free. Box 9.7 has some ideas for good, cheap rewards for kids of different ages.

The magic of star charts

I can hear the groans from here! "Not star charts," I hear you say. "They never work and end up causing more problems

Box 9.7. Cheap (and free) rewards for kids of different ages. Tick the ones that your child might like

- A trip to the park
- Getting to stay up half an hour late
- Getting to choose what sort of take-away to order
- Getting to watch a favourite cartoon
- Getting half an hour on the PlayStation
- Having a friend round to stay overnight
- Having Mum paint your nails
- A small toy (e.g. something from a pound shop)
- A magazine
- A small amount of money (e.g. 20p, or 50p)
- Add some rewards that you think your child will like:

1 ... ...
2 ... ...
3 ... ...
4 ... ...
5 ... ...
6 ... ...

Box.9.8. Dr Drusilla answers your questions about rewards

"Dear Dr Drusilla,

I know I'm supposed to reward my little Horace when he has been brave. But I'm so worried! Won't he become dependent on rewards to get things done? And what on earth will happen when I'm not around to give a reward?
Yours, in desperate search of an answer."

Herbert Hinchliffe, Transylvania

Dr Drusilla says:

"Herbert, be calmed! By rewarding Horace when he does something brave, you are being a wonderful parent. You don't have to keep rewarding a behaviour for ever. Once he has mastered a new brave behaviour, you can phase out the rewards. You can then start to give him rewards for a different or more difficult type of brave behaviour. Besides, children who get lots of praise and rewards when they are little, become very good at praising themselves. So, when they are grown up, they can give themselves a pat on the back if there is no one else around to do it. Keep up the good work Herbert!"

"Dear Dr Drusilla,

I've got a bone to pick with you! My 6 year old Mervyn is just so messy. I wanted him to be more tidy, so I decided to set up a reward scheme just like you said. I told him, if you make your bed, tidy your toys, clear the table, and put away all of the ironing every day, then I will give you a sticker. Well, Dr Drusilla, I'm afraid that your fancy reward schemes don't work. He hasn't done one jot of tidying since. What do you say to that then?"

Timothy Turnpike, Tunbridge Wells

Dr Drusilla says:

"Well Timothy, first of all, I would like to say well done for giving it a go. However, I think you might need to make some little adjustments to your reward scheme. Remember, when we are trying to encourage new behaviours, we have to

Continued

> encourage them little by little. By asking Mervyn to become an ace housekeeper overnight, I'm afraid you were expecting a little bit too much. Perhaps you could start by giving Mervyn a sticker if he has a go at making his bed. When he has cracked that, you can say 'Mervyn, you are so good at making your bed now, I think we should go to the next level of the game. Now you will get a sticker if you make your bed and tidy your toys up.' Also Timothy, I think you need to look at your expectations for your child. It is all well and good to get our children to aim high, but if we set them a target that is too high, we are setting them up for failure. If you are not sure what it is fair to ask of your child, maybe you could ask other parents that you trust, or you could ask Mervyn's teacher. Good luck with your new reward scheme."

than solutions." Well, that's because getting a star chart right is one of the trickiest things that we get parents to do. To get them right, you have to know about a whole load of pitfalls. Unfortunately, most parents (and quite a lot of professionals) are never taught how to do a star chart properly. However, once you know the tricks, they are dead easy, and they work like a charm!

Even if you have had a failed star chart before, have a look at this next section and have one more try ... I think that you might be surprised.

Is a star chart right for my child?

Star charts tend to work best with children aged about four years old and up. Any younger and they can be a bit hit and miss. Star charts can work right up to the early teenage years, although obviously your teenager won't necessarily want it stuck on the fridge for all to see. Also, if you are planning this with a teenager, you will need to make sure that there is nothing childish about it – maybe replacing the stars with just simple ticks.

How to get star charts right

CHOOSE YOUR BEHAVIOUR

Now you need to choose the behaviour that your child is going to get stars for. This can be a good behaviour, e.g. tidying up your room; or it can be a confident behaviour, e.g. sleeping in your own bed all night; or indeed anything else that you want to see more of in your child. Be very careful that you are choosing a behaviour that you want to see more of, not something that you want to see less of. I recently worked with some parents who got in a terrible mess trying to do a star chart for 'not fighting with your sister'. We changed it round so that the child got stars for 'getting on well with your sister' and it worked a treat.

CHOOSE THE REWARD

With star charts, you don't have to give a reward every time your child does a behaviour that you like – instead, they just get a star. Then, when they have enough stars, they get the reward. You need to make sure that the reward is something that really excites them – but again, it need not be something very expensive.

CHOOSE WHEN THEY GET THE REWARD

It is a good idea to make sure that the first reward comes really fast. This really gets kids motivated and excited about keeping the star chart going. I recently worked with a group of families who had young children with anxiety and depression. We asked all of the families to go away and set up a star chart for their kids. The next week, they came back, buzzing with how well it had all worked. All except for one family, The Kellys, who said that it hadn't worked at all. When we asked about the details of what they had done, it turned out that they had told their child that they needed to get 60 stars before they earned their reward. Can you see what the problem was? Another one of the dads in the group saw the problem immediately and suggested that the Kellys change it so that the child got a reward after just three stars. This dad was exactly right; he had pointed out that the Kellys' child was really demotivated. He felt that 60 stars would take so long that he might as well not bother. When the Kellys changed it so that their son only needed three stars, the chart began working really well. As the chart starts to get going, you can gradually increase the number of stars that your child needs to get before they get their reward. However, to begin with, make sure that your child gets a reward really quickly, so that they feel really positive about doing the chart.

MAKE SURE THAT THE FIRST FEW STARS COME REALLY FAST

This is the same point really. As well as making sure that the first rewards come quickly, make sure that the first stars come quickly – within the first day if at all possible. This way, your child will feel excited and positive about doing the chart.

MAKE SURE WHAT YOU ARE ASKING IS MANAGEABLE

I have seen lots of star charts fail because the parents set goals that were too hard for the child. You need to make sure that what you are asking is manageable, or you will get nowhere and everyone will end up fed-up. So, for example, if you want to get your dog-phobic child more confident with dogs, it is no use saying, "Every time you stroke the slavering, 9-stone, bull mastiff that lives next door, you can have a star." You will need to start with something more manageable. For example, "Every time you go into the room where granny keeps her poodle, you will get a star!"

GET THEM INVOLVED

Sometimes kids can be suspicious of what their parents are up to – especially anxious or depressed kids. Sometimes these kids can be quite wary of even nice things, like star charts. So, get them involved. Get them to design or decorate the chart, let them choose a reward (within reason) and let them negotiate how many stars they need to get before they earn the reward.

NEVER, NEVER, *NEVER* MARK UP FAILURES ON A STAR CHART

This is one that lots of people get wrong, even some nameless TV psychologists!

If you mark a failure on the star chart, what is the child going to feel about the chart? Are they going to look at it, stuck on the fridge and think, "Yep, that's me, loads of stars, I'm a really great kid, who is good at achieving things"? No, they are going to see the black marks and failures and, all of a sudden, the wonderful star chart is shouting, loud and clear, what a failure your child is. It's no wonder that parents sometimes tell me that their kids don't like star charts. Once they do it the right way, though, the same parents come back telling me how wonderful star charts are. So, what should you do if your child doesn't manage to get one of their stars? If at all possible, you should ignore it. If you feel that you can't ignore it, then do what you must, but please, please, *please*, don't record it on that star chart!

LEAVE DAYS AND DATES OFF

This is a clever little trick that I only learnt recently, and it's great! Many parents set up their star chart by saying something like: "You get a star every night that you do your homework before 6pm. If you get five stars by Saturday, then we will go and get you that new t-shirt." They then have a chart with the days of the week marked on it, and the kid is supposed to get one star every day until Saturday. Then the kid has a really bad day on Tuesday and doesn't get his star. No problem, you think, maybe he will have a better day tomorrow. The thing is, your kid has now spotted that he can't possibly get five stars by Saturday, so he gives up, and the star chart has failed. However, there is a really easy solution to this problem. Just leave out any mention of days. Just say, "When you have got five stars, we will go and get the t-shirt." It doesn't matter if it takes 5 days or 8 or 18 days, the child can just keep trying until they get there. (Little note: if it looks like it's going to take 18 days, maybe you've set the bar too high. Try making it a bit easier to achieve to start with.)

FOLLOW THE USUAL RULES FOR GIVING THE REWARDS

The rules for giving stars are exactly the same as the rules for ordinary rewards that are summarised in Box 9.9. In particular, make sure that you never take a star or a reward away. Once your child has earned their star or their reward, it is theirs and it can't be taken away. This is very important if the relationship of trust that you are building with your child is to be maintained.

Box 9.9. Summary – ten top tips for great star charts

1. Decide whether a star chart is right for your child. Star charts work particularly well for kids aged 4–12, but can work with older and younger kids too.
2. Choose the behaviour that you want to see more of.
3. Choose the reward.
4. Choose how many stars your child must earn before they get the reward.
5. Make sure that the first few stars come really fast.
6. Make sure that what you are asking is manageable.
7. Get your child involved.
8. Never, never, *never* mark up failures on a star chart.
9. Leave days and dates off the chart.
10. Follow the usual rules for giving the stars and the rewards – see Box 9.6 on page 83.

Box 9.10 on the next page shows an example of a filled-in star chart. You and your child can design you own star charts, or there is a blank copy of this one at the end of the book.

The techniques that we have talked about in this chapter are excellent for encouraging more good behaviour and more brave behaviour. Hopefully by now, your children will be so busy impressing you with their good and brave behaviours, that they won't have any time left for anything else ... However, children are designed to do things that sometimes try our patience. Chapter 10 gives you some ideas for dealing with just these sorts of behaviours.

So, do take your time here, and don't be in too much of a hurry to move on. The tips given in chapter 10 will work much better if you have cracked everything in this chapter first. Indeed, if your child is not getting all of the attention that they need by behaving well and by being confident, no amount of effort will make the techniques in chapter 10 work. When you are feeling confident at spotting good and brave behaviours, and are getting good at giving praise for them, you are ready to move on to chapter 10.

Summary of Chapter Nine

- This chapter has been designed to help you to get the behaviours you want from your child, with the minimum fuss and tears. Using these techniques will also help you to build up your child's Seven Confident Thoughts. This chapter should have:

  ⟹ Helped you to decide what good behaviours and brave behaviours you want to see more of

  ⟹ Given you top tips for getting more of these behaviours, using

    ⟹ Praise

    ⟹ Rewards

    ⟹ Star Charts

STAR CHART

This star chart belongs to: **Sam**

I will get a star every time that I: **Go to the toilet on my own**

When I have got........**5**........stars, I will get a treat.

My treat is..............**I can spend £2 at the pound shop**

10

On their best behaviour: getting your kids to do what you want without tears and tantrums

Part 2: Getting less bad behaviour and less anxious behaviour

Many parents of anxious or depressed kids get very frustrated by the comments that they get from other people, such as: "What a good little boy!" or "What a well-behaved young lady she is!" Whilst their children are often on their best behaviour when they are out of the safety of their own homes, they can be complete horrors within their own families. This chapter gives you some suggestions for dealing head-on with the difficult behaviours that all children, including anxious and depressed ones, often display.

When we see parents in our clinics, we always teach the ways of increasing good behaviours before we go on to dealing with the less desirable behaviours. I have done this in the careful ordering of this book too. Some parents find this frustrating. A frequent plea in the early stages of our parent groups is "When are you going to tell us how to deal with the really annoying behaviours – that's what we really want to hear." However, after a few weeks of trying the techniques for getting more good and more brave behaviour, parents start coming in with marvellous stories. One parent recently said to me, "I can't believe it, I haven't even started dealing with Jordan's fighting, and yet it's almost completely gone away – he's a changed boy!" The reason for this is obvious when you think about it. When kids can get nice, positive interactions from their parents by being good, they have less interest in getting your attention by being bad.

However, many families find that even after doing all of the positive parenting stuff – spending time with their kids, playing, praising, rewarding, and so on – their children are still showing some behaviours that parents want to change.

In the past, most parents who come to our clinic have dealt with these behaviours by shouting or by smacking, or by using some other harsh type of punishment. By the time they have been to our groups for a few weeks though, they are starting to recognise that these techniques don't work well and are really damaging for anxious or depressed kids. So what techniques can parents use instead? This chapter will talk about three skills for parents: Ignoring, Time Out, and Consequences. However, do not move on to these techniques until you are sure that your child is able to get all of the attention that they want and need by being good and being confident. If they have not yet learnt how to get this attention and reassurance from you by being good, then the techniques in this chapter will not work.

Ignoring

As you will now be gathering, the one thing that all kids want (and need) is attention from adults, and especially from their parents. This need is even greater for anxious and depressed kids. This can be a real pain, but as a smart parent you can really turn it to your advantage.

In the last chapter we talked about how praise can be used to increase good and confident behaviours. Why is praise so good for this? Praise is a form of really good, strong attention from parents and, if a behaviour wins your kid some attention, you can guarantee that they will do it again and again.

Helpfully for us, it also works the other way around. If a behaviour doesn't get any attention, then you can be sure that your kid will get very bored with it, pretty soon. So, we teach the technique of *ignoring* to the parents who come along to us. Some of them are a bit sceptical to start with, but once they get the hang of it, there's no stopping them. A funny little case example is described in the case study below.

James was seven and, as well as being an anxious boy, he had a bit of a hot temper. In particular, he had learned some rather rude words at school and delighted in displaying these linguistic skills in polite company. Whenever his mother annoyed him (by not letting him do just as he liked), he would swear profanely. His mother, horribly embarrassed, would tell him off. When we explained about the attention rule, James' mother decided to give ignoring a go. So, whenever James swore, she was to turn away from him, not say a word, not look at him, and ignore him totally until he had calmed down. She knew that it was going to be hard – really hard – because she was so embarrassed by James' behaviour, but she decided that since the swearing was not actually doing any harm she was going to have a go at ignoring. When she came back the next week she told us that the first two days had been awful – she had ignored James' swearing really well – but it was almost as if he just tried harder to get her attention. But she stuck at it and by day three the swearing was getting less and less. By day four it had almost gone completely and, for the last three days, James had not sworn at all.

The rules for Ignoring

WHEN CAN I USE IGNORING?

You can use ignoring for almost any behaviour that you don't like. It is especially good for moaning, whingeing, nagging, tantrums, and swearing.

WHEN CAN'T I USE IGNORING?

The only time when you shouldn't use ignoring is if the behaviour is dangerous and someone might get hurt. Also, don't use ignoring if your child's behaviour might be damaging things (unless it is their own things, of course. They can make their own choices about that.)

SO WHAT DO I DO?

- Once you have decided that you are going to ignore a behaviour (like the swearing in the case study on page 97), try really hard to ignore it every time that it happens – it will clear up much more quickly than if you only ignore it some of the time.
- When you are ignoring:

  - Don't look at your child
  - Don't talk to your child
  - Don't touch your child

- It is usually best to turn away from your child and focus on something else – go and do some tidying up, or pick up a magazine. If necessary, even go in to a different room, leaving the child where they are.
- As soon as your child starts behaving well, praise them for the good behaviour and stop the ignoring.
- If the unwanted behaviour starts up again, start your ignoring again.

SOME THINGS TO WATCH OUT FOR

Beware! It may get worse before it gets better

- When you first begin using ignoring, your child won't know that you mean it and at first will try even harder to get your attention. PERSEVERE ... it will be worth it.

Make sure you really are ignoring

- One of the most common mistakes that parents make is that they start talking to their child halfway through ... I have even heard parents say to their child, "I'm ignoring you ... I'm not listening." Of course, the moment you do this, the child knows that they have your attention and you are scuppered.

Learn to make snap decisions

- If you have a stubborn child, the first few times of ignoring a bad behaviour can be very tiring. Unfortunately, if parents give in after they have been ignoring for a while, they are just teaching their children that if they are persistent in their bad behaviour, they will eventually get the attention that they want – and no one wants to teach their children that! This means that if you give in, your job will be more difficult the next time. For this reason, we always teach parents to make a snap decision about whether they can follow through the ignoring or not. If you decide that you are not feeling tough enough to ignore something to the bitter end, give in straight away!

Don't do it for the first time in Tesco

- Ignoring is really hard to do, but it does get easier with practice. The first time you try it, it will probably be very, very hard. So, make sure that you've got everything on your side when you first give this a go. For instance, it is perhaps best if you don't have your first go at ignoring on a Saturday morning in Tesco! Try it when you are at home when you have plenty of time and are feeling calm and in control.

Box 10.1 contains sections of the Agony Column that we give to parents to help them get to grips with ignoring.

Box 10.1. Dr Drusilla deals with Ignoring

"Dear Dr Drusilla,

I've been hearing all about this new-fangled way of controlling unwanted behaviour in children – this so-called 'ignoring'. Well I think it's a disgrace! I'm not going to just stand by while my children swear and curse and answer back. They will think they can get away with anything!"

Disgusted and Horrified, Derby

Dr Drusilla replies:

"Dear Disgusted and Horrified,

You are right – we have to teach our children what behaviour is wrong, and I'm sure that your children know there are rules about not swearing and answering back. Now what you have to do is teach them that they cannot get what they want by swearing or answering back. And what do children want ...? That's right – ATTENTION! So we have to teach them that they get absolutely NO attention for this sort of behaviour. So, when they whinge and moan and answer back, the best thing to do is ignore them completely. They won't think they can get away with it – on the contrary, they will find the ignoring most irritating and will soon give up their moaning! Also, by keeping calm when your children are nagging, you are providing a very positive example for them."

"Dear Dr Drusilla,

I think this ignoring thing is a really good idea, but the problem is – I'm useless at it. I can ignore the nagging for about five minutes, but then it just gets to me and I explode at my kids. I'm so hopeless, what can I do?"

Cinderella Snotkopf, Stoke on Trent

Continued

Dr Drusilla replies:

"Dear Cinders,

Well first of all, you can stop telling yourself that you are hopeless! Telling yourself that you are no good will just be getting you down, and that won't help at all. Ignoring is one of the hardest skills to learn, and I am impressed that you have been trying so hard. However, you are right – ignoring for a few minutes and then giving in can do more harm than good. It teaches your children that if they keep nagging and moaning for long enough, they will get what they want! So, I will let you into a little secret Cinderella – when I have to deal with a moaning child, I decide whether I am feeling strong enough to ignore until the bitter end. If I'm not feeling up to it, I give in straight away. If I decide to go with the ignoring, I stick it out until the child has stopped moaning. Hang in there Cinders."

Dealing with dangerous and destructive behaviours: Time Out

So, ignoring works really well for annoying but harmless behaviours, but what do you do for those dangerous, aggressive behaviours that might leave someone, or something hurt? One good way of dealing with this is Time Out. You may have heard of Time Out. You may even have tried it. You may even be groaning as you read. But do read on. Time Out is a tricky technique and if you've not been taught properly, it is easy to get wrong. However, with a few simple rules it can become a very gentle and effective way of disciplining an anxious or depressed child. Time Out is best for kids aged about 18 months to 10 years. It is less effective with older children and teenagers, and you will find 'ignoring' and 'consequences' more useful.

Overview of Time Out

Time Out is like super-ignoring. If your child does something dangerous or destructive, they get put in a quiet and boring place for a few minutes to calm down and think about their actions.

HOW TO DO TIME OUT

1. Choose an area where your child will sit for Time Out. Make sure that it is a really boring place – don't use their bedroom as there are interesting things there, and anyway bedrooms should be associated with nice times. Some parents use the stairs or the bathroom. However, do make sure that you choose a safe place.
2. Give your child one warning before you do Time Out. Tell them what they are doing wrong and give them a chance to stop. Warn them that if they don't behave they will have to go to Time Out. So, for example, if your child is fighting, you can say, "Play nicely with your brother, or you will have to sit on the stairs!"
3. If your child doesn't stop, do Time Out straight away. Explain that you are taking them to Time Out because what they did was wrong or dangerous and not allowed. If necessary, take them firmly and calmly by the arm and make them go to Time Out.
4. After this, keep your attention to a minimum in Time Out. Don't look at them, talk to them or touch them unless you have to.
5. If your child is 5 or over, keep them in Time Out for 5 minutes. If they are younger than 5, keep them in Time Out for one minute for each year of their life. So, if they are three, they stay for three minutes, if they are four, they stay for four minutes, etc. Sometimes children leave Time Out before their time is up. Stay calm and return the child until their time is up.
6. Stay nearby in Time Out, to keep an eye on them, but make sure that this doesn't turn into giving attention.
7. Tell them when their time is up. If they say they don't want to come out, just leave them there.

8. Immediately praise the next good thing your child does after they come out.

Sometimes children say that they like Time Out, but don't be fooled by this – it will still be teaching them which behaviours are wrong. That said, if they really do seem to like it, make sure that this is not because they are doing something fun during the Time Out – like watching TV or reading a magazine.

SPECIAL NOTE: TIME OUT AND ANXIOUS CHILDREN

If you have an anxious child, you can still use Time Out – it works really well. However, take a couple of things into account:

1. Make sure that you don't put them somewhere that they are scared during Time Out. Time Out is not meant to be scary, it is just meant to be boring. Don't ever lock a child in a room and always let them keep the light on.
2. Don't let your child use Time Out to get out of doing things that they are scared of.

In Box 10.2, Dr Drusilla deals with some parents' queries about Time Out.

Box 10.2. Dr Drusilla deals with Time Out

"Dear Dr Drusilla,

I like this Time Out business, it has really helped my little Semolina to stop biting. For some reason though, it won't work at all with my son. Little Simeon is scared of dogs and we have been trying to get him used to them. The next step is to stroke next door's Rottweiler. However, every time I tell him to do it, he refuses. I have sent him to Time Out ten times now for refusing to do it, and still he won't go near little Fluffy!

Arabella Splatt, Leighton Buzzoff

Continued

Dr Drusilla replies:

"Dear Arabella,

I am so glad that you are trying to get Simeon used to dogs. But Simeon has clearly got stuck. I wonder if what you are asking is too hard? Perhaps the latest step is just too big! Even us psychologists get it wrong sometimes you know! Try making the step smaller – maybe he just has to go in the same room as Fluffy to start with. Also, I wonder if he likes Time Out because it gets him out of having to see Fluffy? Have you tried using rewards to get Simeon to be brave with dogs? Rewards should always be tried before you resort to Time Out. Good luck Arabella, and don't give up!"

"Dear Dr Drusilla,

I've tried and tried with this Time Out but it's not working and I'm absolutely exhausted. I started by giving Time Out for five minutes, like you said, but that didn't work – she said she LIKED being in Time Out. So, I started making it longer. On Saturday we ran out of time to do anything else because Beryl was in Time Out for nearly three hours."

Herbertina Bunyon, Piddle in the Marsh

Dr Drusilla replies:

"Dear Herbertina,

You poor thing, you really are trying very hard. But don't give up just yet. With just a few little tweaks, you will have Time Out working a treat. First, we shouldn't always believe the little tikes when they say they enjoy Time Out. They do tell fibs some-times – so as not to give us the satisfaction of winning! That said, do have a little think about the place that you use for Time Out – is there any reason why she might really be enjoying it – is there something nice to play with, or a book or a television perhaps? If so, time to think of somewhere else. When you have chosen the right Time Out area, just ignore Beryl when she says she enjoys it. Once her five minutes is up, let her out. I think you will find it starts working pretty soon. There is no need to keep going for three hours – that will probably just make her angry and irritable – not what a busy mum wants!"

Dealing with non-compliance: Consequences

Time Out is great for more serious aggressive behaviours but should be kept to a minimum. If you use it too much it loses its power. Also, it doesn't work so well with older children and teenagers. Ignoring is great for dealing with irritating behaviours, but what about times when your child is refusing to do something that you want them to do. Can you use ignoring for this? Well, of course, the answer is no. If you ask them to do something, "Please go and tidy your room now" and then ignore them, what are the chances that they will actually go and tidy their room ...?

So, for times when your child is non-compliant, or if you find yourself using Time Out too often, another technique to use is one that we call 'consequences'. However, do remember to try all of the positive techniques first – does your child know that they will get praised if they do as they are told? Can you offer a small reward to your child if they do as they are told?

Overview of Consequences

Consequences is when your child is told that if they don't do as they are told, they will lose a privilege. Consequences is suitable for all ages of children and teenagers, but some very young children (under four) may find it more difficult to understand.

HOW TO DO CONSEQUENCES

1. Give your child a warning before you impose the consequence; for example, "Go and put your bike in the garage now, or you won't be allowed to ride your bike for the rest of the day."
2. Only give one warning. If they don't do as they are told, then they get the consequence. "You have not put your bike away, so you cannot ride it for the rest of the day."

3. Try to make the consequence as soon as possible – straight away or the same day. The younger the child is, the more important this is. If you make the consequence something that happens much later (e.g. "You can't go swimming next weekend"), then by the time you get there, the child will have forgotten what the consequence is for and you may well find yourself letting them off the hook.

4. Never give a consequence that is harsh, or cruel, or frightening. It should be something that will annoy the child, but not really distress them, or scare them.

5. Never give a consequence that takes away the child's basic rights; for example, never say "Because you didn't tidy up, you can't go to school today" or "... you're going to bed without dinner."

6. Make sure the consequence is one that you can stick to.

7. Once you have made up your mind, stick to it! If you let your child out of a consequence, they will think that they can get away with non-compliance.

8. Don't worry if your child appears not to care about the consequence – kids often try to look as if they are not bothered, even when they really are.

9. Once you have given the consequence, or at least told the child what the consequence is, stop being annoyed with your child. Remember to praise them straight away when they do something good. This is very, very important for anxious and depressed children.

Box 10.3 has some ideas for good consequences, and for ones that are not so good (all of the bad ones are ones that I have heard parents try, with disastrous results!)

Section Two of this book has given you a number of skills for increasing good and confident behaviours. This chapter has given you techniques for decreasing some of the annoying behaviours that all children display, in a way that is good for anxious

Box 10.3. Good Consequences and Bad Consequences

Good Consequences

- "The TV gets turned off for half an hour."
- "There will be no more PlayStation for the rest of the day."
- "You can't watch the match on TV this afternoon."
- "We will have to leave the park and go home now."
- "You will have to do some extra chores around the house" (but make sure that this is something that you know you can make them do).
- "You will have no sweets on the way home from school today."

Bad Consequences

- "We will cut our holiday short and go home right now."
- "You will go straight to bed now."
- "I will tell your father when he gets home."
- "I will give your pet cat away."
- "You won't go on the school trip next week."
- "You will be grounded for a fortnight."
- "You won't get any dinner."

Can you think why each of these might lead to problems?
Answers in Box 10.4

Box 10.4. Answers to Bad Consequences quiz

We will cut our holiday short and go home right now.

This is bad because it is an empty threat – it is almost impossible to follow through. This leads to the child not believing the parents' threats, which is not a situation you want to get into. If you did decide to stick to your guns and follow it through (I knew one family who did just this) then it ends up being an enormous punishment, out of all proportion with the crime, and not just for the child, but for the whole family. In this family, it led to huge resentment and anger and it took the whole family a long time to trust each other again.

Continued

You will go straight to bed now.

Two problems with this one. First, bed should be a nice place that feels relaxing and pleasant. If bed is used as a punishment, the child will start to feel bad about going to bed and can end up with sleeping problems. Second, especially if it is used before night time, it can be well out of proportion with the crime – it ends up being a very long Time Out.

I will tell your father when he gets home.

Lots of problems here. First, it means that the consequence doesn't happen straightaway and, in fact, the child doesn't know what the consequence is going to be – so they are worrying about it for the rest of the day. Second, it sets Dad up as the 'big bad wolf', which is not good for his relationship with the child. Third, it teaches the child that Mum can't cope with his/her behaviour. Fourth, by the time Dad gets home, Mum has usually forgotten and so nothing actually happens. Finally, Dad was not there when the offence occurred, so really isn't the best one to deal with it. In fact, Dad is usually just wanting to come in and have a sit down, and is unlikely to be in the mood for dealing calmly and rationally with bad behaviour. So, he will either over-react totally, or do nothing at all.

I will give your pet cat away.

Unless this is given because the child really isn't looking after the cat properly, it is cruel to use this as a consequence. It will lead to serious upset for the child and resentment toward the parent. These things are especially bad for anxious and depressed kids (remember the Seven Confident Thoughts? See Box 7.1 on page 59).

You won't go on the school trip next week.

Two things here. First, it is too far away to be really good as a consequence. By the time it comes round a younger child will have forgotten what the consequence is for (so it won't work to help their behaviour improve) and an older child will feel really resentful towards you for a whole week, which is not good when you are trying to create a calm family atmosphere. Second, it is quite harsh, and potentially humiliating for the child.

Continued

You will be grounded for a fortnight.
Several problems here. First, it is very harsh. Second, will this parent really be able to keep it up? What does the child learn if the parent caves in after a day or two? Finally, the household will be tense and resentful, which is problematic, especially for sensitive kids.

You won't get any dinner.
It is always unacceptable for a parent to take away a child's basic rights, even if they have been really naughty. Denying a child food, school, medical attention, or sleep should never, never be used ... unless you want a little visit from Social Services!

---

and depressed children. Once you are fairly confident in these skills you are ready to try the techniques described in chapter 11 for dealing with fears and worries.

Summary of Chapter Ten

- This chapter gives you tips for cutting down the last bits of naughty behaviour and anxious behaviour that are left when you have given all of the positive techniques (e.g. praise and reward) your very best shot.

➡ Ignoring

- *This can be used for any annoying behaviours that are not posing a threat to people or property.*
- Try to ignore the annoying behaviour every time it occurs.
- When ignoring the behaviour, try not to look at, touch or speak to your child, unless you absolutely have to.
- As soon as your child stops doing the annoying thing, praise them warmly straightaway.
- The behaviour will probably get a bit worse before it gets better, but hang in there.

➡ Time Out

- *This can be used for more serious behaviours that are dangerous or destructive.*
- Put the child in a safe, boring place.
- Make them stay there until Time Out is over, and you say that they can come out. This is one minute for each year of the child's age, up to a maximum of five minutes.
- Ignore them during the Time Out.
- Take note of special precautions for anxious children when using Time Out:
  - Make sure they are not scared by the place you do Time Out.
  - Make sure that in doing Time Out, they are not getting out of doing the thing that they are afraid of.
  - Keep use of Time Out to a minimum. Only use it for really serious behaviours.
- After Time Out, praise the next good or confident behaviour that you see.

➡ Consequences

- *Consequences can be used for times when your child is non-compliant, or for dangerous behaviours if you feel you are using Time Out too much.*
- Give one warning and then, if you don't get the behaviour that you want, give the child the consequence.
- Give the consequence as soon as you possibly can.
- Make the consequence mild, appropriate and make sure it is not something that is scary, or removing a basic right.
- Once you've given a consequence, stick to it.
- Once the consequence is over, forget about it, and give your child praise for some good behaviour as soon as ever you can.

11

Dealing with fears and worries

Fears and worries are common in childhood. For example, think of all of the children that you know. Can you think of a single one who has not gone through a period of separation anxiety? (Separation anxiety is when the child gets upset when they are parted from their main caregiver.) It is completely normal for young children to go through this phase, starting from about 8 months old. In fact, it would be more unusual if a child did not go through it. Likewise, it is really common for pre-school children to have fears of monsters, ghosts, the dark, and the like. Older children tend to develop mild fears of animals, such as dogs or spiders, and it is very common for teenagers to become preoccupied with their appearance and their social standing at school.

These fears and worries appear for a reason. Psychologists now think that such fears have an evolutionary purpose. If a young child screams when he is separated from his mother this means that, if she really has lost him, then she has a good chance of hearing the screams and will be able to find him again.

Likewise, teenagers are at the point where they are beginning to become a bit more independent from their families. So, this is the time when they need to hone their skills for getting along with other people. If they are worried about how well-liked they are, then this will spur them on to getting some good social skills. Similarly, teenagers are reaching the start of their fertile period. In the past, those who worried about their appearance would have taken most care of their looks and would have been the ones who snapped up the best partners and had the most children. Of course, nowadays we don't really want our teenagers breeding from the age of 15, but that is what our bodies were designed to do, and so that is what our worries are designed to make us think about.

That said, no matter how useful some fears and worries can be, if we have too much of them they can get to be a real pain. In this chapter, I will give tips for dealing with fears and worries.

Fears

So, fears are really common in childhood but happily most children seem to grow out of them. Why do some children not grow out of them? Well, we think the answer to this is quite complicated, but a big part of it lies in two important processes which psychologists call 'avoidance' and the 'fight-flight' response.

Avoidance

We know that very often when sensitive children encounter something that is frightening, they back away from it. Usually well-meaning parents help them to do this. So, for instance, a kindly parent will often tell me that they let their child sleep in bed with them because the child is so frightened of sleeping on their own. However, this kindness can bring some problems with it. The thing is, by not facing the thing that they are afraid of, children do not get to test out whether it is really scary or not.

For instance, a child who never sleeps in their own bed, never finds out that the monsters under the bed won't come out and eat you in the middle of the night! Second, by helping the child to avoid the thing that they are scared of, the parent is sometimes giving a subtle message that, "yes, sleeping on your own really is dangerous". So, this is what psychologists call avoidance, and it is a real key to understanding anxiety. The case study below shows how avoidance can make fears turn into phobias.

Miranda was 12 years old when her parents took her to see a psychologist because of her fear of snakes. This is a very common fear and not one that usually causes big problems for people living in the U.K. However, Miranda lived in a rural area where there were particularly large numbers of grass snakes and her fear had got so bad that she could no longer go outside. The fear had started when Miranda was much younger. She had seen something on TV about people getting bitten by snakes and this had really worried her. A few days later she was out for a walk with her parents and she saw a grass snake. She became really upset and her dad ended up picking her up and carrying her home. From then onwards, Miranda made a real fuss about going near where she had seen the snake, and if they went anywhere near there her dad ended up carrying her. Eventually, the fuss got too much for the family, and they avoided walking near that area at all. As time went by Miranda's fear got worse; she refused to go for family walks at all, especially at the time of year when most snakes were around. If her family managed to drag her out on walks, they would usually be cut short when Miranda got upset.

Can you see how Miranda's fear turned into a phobia? Her kind-hearted family knew that the snakes could not harm Miranda, but they didn't like to see her upset (and if truth be known, her mum didn't like snakes much either) and so they let her stay out of the way of snakes. Over time, Miranda built up a whole load of fears about what would happen if she came across a snake – it would bite her, it would get in her hair and clothes and that she would be so scared she would be sick. Of course, none of this was true, but Miranda had no opportunity to find this out. In Box 11.1, we see how Miranda's treatment progressed.

As you can see from Miranda's treatment, it is very rare that a

Box 11.1. Treating Miranda

After spending a bit of time getting to know each other, Deirdre the psychologist and Miranda set about developing a 'fear hierarchy'. A fear hierarchy is a list of the things that you are scared of (in this case, to do with snakes) starting with the least scary thing at the bottom, and the most scary thing at the top.

Miranda's hierarchy looked like this:

- Step 9. Holding a live snake
- Step 8. Touching a live snake
- Step 7. Looking at a live snake
- Step 6. Being in a room with a live snake
- Step 5. Looking at a snake on TV
- Step 4. Looking at photographs of a snake
- Step 3. Looking at realistic drawings of a snake
- Step 2. Looking at cartoon drawings of a snake
- Step 1. Looking at really bad stick drawings of a snake

To begin with, Deirdre drew some very bad, scribbly drawings of snakes because Miranda thought that she would feel brave enough to look at these. Miranda felt a bit uncomfortable but she did manage to sit and look at the pictures. Deirdre got her to sit and look at them for 15 minutes. At the end of the 15 minutes, Miranda said that she felt fine – she didn't feel uncomfortable with the pictures any more. This process of getting over feelings of discomfort by spending time with the fear is known as 'habituation' and is very, very effective. Next, Deirdre got Miranda to look at some cartoon pictures of a snake that they found in a children's book. After

Continued

15 minutes, Miranda said that she was feeling fine. Over the next few weeks, Miranda and Deirdre, helped by Miranda's family, worked their way up the fear hierarchy. For the last few steps, Miranda's dad arranged for Miranda to go to his colleague's house. His colleague kept a snake as a pet and agreed that she could go and see it. Although she felt really scared, she was very brave and managed to work right up her fear hierarchy to the very top – even managing to hold the snake for a few minutes. Miranda had conquered her fear and was able to go outside without being terrified that she would meet a grass snake! Her family helped make sure that her phobia didn't come back by making sure that she had lots of opportunities for meeting grass snakes, and so for finding out that they would not harm her.

psychologist would recommend that a child should drop their avoidance and just face up to their worst fears straight away. This is how fears used to be treated in the past – someone who was scared of spiders might be put in a room with lots of spiders. However, we now know that this often does more harm than good and, wherever possible, people are encouraged to drop their avoidance little bit by little bit.

The Fight-Flight Response

This is another psychological process that we think is very involved in fears and phobias. I would like you to think back in time, to the era when human beings lived in caves ... You are a little caveman, out hunting for your lunch ... but unfortunately, you are not the only thing looking for lunch and, just as you round a corner, you bump into an enormous, very hungry, sabre-toothed tiger! What do you do? Well in that circumstance most people would do the same thing – run away as fast as they possibly can. In order to run away from the tiger, our bodies need to get themselves ready for action. So we start pumping out adrenalin: this makes our hearts pump blood to our muscles, our lungs start breathing in lots of oxygen, and makes our brain work at 90 miles per hour. Meanwhile, all of that blood getting pumped to our muscles, so that we can run fast, has got to come from somewhere. So the little caveman's body takes blood away from his stomach and away from his skin – those parts can do without for a while. Unfortunately, all of this body-busyness has some unpleasant side effects – it can feel *awful*. The caveman's legs feel shaky, his breathing is shallow and fast, he feels sick and his stomach is churning, his head feels fuzzy and he might be sweating, he looks pale and ill ... Does all of this remind you of anything? Well done if you spotted that this is exactly how your child looks when they are very afraid. This is because, despite living in the twenty-first century, our poor old bodies are still designed for the stone age. We don't have to face sabre-toothed tigers any more – we have to face school, and crowds of people, and homework, and dark toilets, and so on. Unfortunately, our bodies and our brains have really not caught up, and we still respond to our fears in exactly the same way as the little caveman – by getting ready to run away.

There is really not much that we can do about this. This is the way that our bodies are designed and we just have to put up with it. However, it is very important for children, and their parents, to understand that all of these feelings that they get cannot hurt them at all. These feelings are just our bodies getting ready to go for a big run ... and you don't see many unhealthy marathon runners, do you? Although your child may look and feel absolutely terrible when they are scared, they are not doing themselves any harm at all. They are completely safe, and need to be reassured of this.

Also, lots of people feel as if they are going to faint when they are scared. This is because of the altered blood flow in the body and the brain, but actually, this is the one time when you absolutely *cannot* faint. Your blood pressure is temporarily very high when you are scared, and you can't faint when your blood pressure is raised.[1]

Tips for dealing with fears

Getting over a fear or phobia needs to be done gently and slowly, but is really fairly simple.

1. Draw up a 'fear hierarchy' with your child, like Miranda and Deirdre did. There is a blank worksheet for this in Box 11.2.
2. Make sure that the steps from one level to the next are little ones. If you make a step too big your child might not make it. If in doubt, make really tiny steps. It doesn't matter if there are 4 levels or 44, as long as each step is small enough for your child to manage.
3. Begin with level one.
4. Get your child to stay with the fear for 15 minutes. Miranda stayed with the drawings of the snake for 15 minutes. Reassure your child that even though they might feel terrible, they are just fine, and will feel better in a few minutes.
5. After your child has managed this level, give them loads and loads of praise. Also, think about giving them a small reward.
6. If your child is ready, move onto the next level. Do exactly the same as before.
7. If your child is looking tired or fed up, leave the next step to another time.

Little things to remember:

---

[1] There is one rare exception, which is that some people with a blood phobia do faint if they see blood. In this case, something unusual happens to the blood pressure – it falls, and they can faint. However, if this has never happened to your child, it is unlikely to start now and you should feel comfortable reassuring them that they are fine, and cannot faint.

Box 11.2. Draw a fear hierarchy for one of your child's fears

- Step 10 … … … … … … … … … … … … … … …
- Step 9 … … … … … … … … … … … … … … … …
- Step 8 … … … … … … … … … … … … … … … …
- Step 7 … … … … … … … … … … … … … … … …
- Step 6 … … … … … … … … … … … … … … … …
- Step 5 … … … … … … … … … … … … … … … …
- Step 4 … … … … … … … … … … … … … … … …
- Step 3 … … … … … … … … … … … … … … … …
- Step 2 … … … … … … … … … … … … … … … …
- Step 1 … … … … … … … … … … … … … … … …

Tips:
- Start by filling in Step 1. Make this something really easy.
- Then do Step 10. Make this the final goal.
- Fill in the steps in between. Make each step just a tiny bit harder than the one below it.
- There don't have to be 10 steps, there could be 3 or 20, or anything in between.

- When your child is doing this, they will really be relying on you for support. So, whatever you do, be positive. Don't criticise them at all, even if they are being whingey or slow. You need to be really, really patient. If you are not feeling in a patient mood, this is not the time to do the fear hierarchy. Get someone else to do it, or leave it for another time.
- Your child will be looking to you for 'safety signs'. Anxious kids do this all of the time – they don't even know that they are doing it, but they are constantly looking at *you* to see if *you* think that the situation is safe. If you are looking terrified or tearful, they will interpret this as, "oh no, Mum is scared – it MUST be dangerous". This is a bad thing! So, if you are not

feeling happy, you need to really fake it here! Big confident smile, calm voice, and off you go!

TROUBLESHOOTING, OR "MY CHILD WON'T DO IT"

- Are the steps too big? Think about making the steps even smaller.
- Is the reward working? What reward are you offering in return for your child's bravery? Talk to them, and see if this needs to be changed.
- Get someone else to try – favourite aunty, big admired brother, etc.

TOP TIP

Combine your child's fear hierarchy with a star chart. For example, every time your child moves one level up their fear hierarchy, they get a star towards a big reward. However, you may need to also give a little reward at each level, to make sure that the momentum is kept up. Good ideas for really effective star charts are given in chapter 9.

Worries

We all worry. It is really quite normal. It is important to remember this and to be aware that worry, no matter how bad it feels, really can't hurt you. Common sayings such as "I was going mad with worry" and "he worried himself to death" give worrying a bad name. Worrying can't make you go mad and it can't kill you. However, excessive worrying can feel unpleasant, and if you have a child who seems to worry about everything, all of the time, then this section gives you some tips on how to deal with this.

I am going to split worrying into two types. Each one has a slightly different solution. I call them realistic worries, and unrealistic worries. Realistic worries are the sort of everyday worries that crop up about real problems that we are facing. So, for instance, a child who struggles at school might worry that they are going to fail a test. A child who has suffered teasing or bullying might be worried about being bullied when they go in to school tomorrow. Basically, if the worry stands a reasonable chance of coming true, then I call it a 'realistic worry'. However, not all worries fall into this camp. If you have an anxious or depressed child, then the chances are that many of their worries will be 'unrealistic' worries. These are worries that are very unlikely to be true. An unrealistic worry might be "if I fail my test then my teacher will hit me", or "all of the kids at school hate me", or "if I go to the dentist, it will really hurt me".

Dealing with realistic worries

The best way to deal with realistic worries is to sit down with your child and work out what you can do to solve the problem that they are facing. For example, if they are scared of failing a test then you could work out a revision plan (perhaps with some little rewards built in). If they are scared of being teased, then you can help to solve the problem by talking to school, and coming up with some strategies for dealing with the teasing. Sometimes these worries are just problems that feel too big for an anxious or depressed child. In the case study opposite, Katy has a worry like this. In this case, you and your child need to sit down with a piece of paper and break the problem into little bits that are more manageable.

Dealing with unrealistic worries

Sometimes we worry about things that are just not likely to come true. For instance, lots of kids worry that if they do badly on a test or on their homework, their teacher will shout at them. Whilst it is true that their teacher might be disappointed, and might want to talk to your child to try and work out where the problem is, teachers nowadays should really not be shouting at

Katy was twelve years old and was really worried about a big science test that she was going to have at school. Her mum knew that Katy would be just fine, as long as she did a little bit of revision. However, in all of the worrying Katy just didn't seem to know what to do to solve the problem. So, Katy and her mum sat down and wrote a list of what Katy needed to do to solve her problem. It looked like this:

1. Look in homework book, to see what the test was going to be on
2. Write a list of the topics that Katy needed to revise
3. Split the topics up so that she had one or two to look at each night between now and the test
4. Each night sit down for half an hour and read through that night's topic(s)
5. Each night get Mum to give Katy a five minute quiz on the topics she had read through
6. Each night, after the quiz, Katy to watch MTV for half an hour as a treat

Katy's mum was keen for Katy to learn solutions to her own problems, so she didn't just write this list for Katy. Instead, she helped Katy to do it, but encouraged her to come up with her own solution as much as possible. It was Mum's excellent idea to build in a little reward each night as a treat for Katy working so hard.

children for poor work. If you think that your child's teacher is doing this, then see chapter 13 and consider having a word with school. So, if you know that the worry is unrealistic, either because (a) your child always does better than they think or (b) you know that the teacher won't shout, what can you do?

The best thing to do here is to get your child to test out their worries. Jo has a worry like this in the case study on page 122.

Jo's mum did just the right thing. She realised that Jo often thought that she was going to get into trouble and that this was unrealistic. She wanted Jo to test out her fears. Box 11.3 has the

Jo was 10 years old when she was referred to us for problems with anxiety and mild depression. She was very tearful going anywhere without her mother and was very unhappy at school, despite having an understanding and caring teacher. Jo's mum went on a short course on 'parenting an anxious child' at the local hospital. During the course, she learnt some of the techniques that we talk about in this book including how to deal with worries.

One night Jo came home in floods of tears. Her teacher had taught them some new grammar skills that day, and had set some homework on the topic. Some of the children had not been concentrating and the teacher had said that she expected everyone to do very well in the homework. The teacher had clearly not meant Jo, who always worked hard, but Jo was now convinced that if she got any of her homework wrong, then her teacher would shout at her. Jo's mum sat her down and listened to her concerns. She found out exactly what Jo was worried about. Jo was convinced that if she made a mistake her teacher would shout at her and possibly smack her, and that she would cry. After she had listened, and Jo had calmed down a bit, Jo and her mum hatched a plan. Jo's mum knew that the teacher wouldn't shout and that she certainly wouldn't smack Jo so she persuaded Jo that they needed to test out the worry. In order to do this, they would put a mistake in the homework on purpose to test out whether the teacher would smack and shout. Jo wasn't convinced that this was a good idea but her mum said that if she did it, they would go to the shop after school and Jo could have a treat (some day-glo nail varnish that she had her eye on). Jo reluctantly agreed. The next day Mum picked Jo up from school. Jo was all smiles. Mum asked Jo whether her worry had come true. Did the teacher smack or shout? Did Jo cry? Of course, the answer to all of the questions was "no". Jo got her luminous nail varnish, and everyone was happy. More importantly, Jo had learnt a valuable lesson – sometimes our worries play tricks on us and tell us that bad things might happen when, in fact, they are not going to happen at all.

Box 11.3. Testing out unrealistic worries with your child

a. Find out what your child thinks is going to happen. From Jo's story opposite, Jo was worried that if she made a mistake her teacher would be cross.

b. Find out *exactly* why that would be so bad for your child. Jo was scared that the teacher would shout or even hit her, and that she, Jo, would end up in tears.

c. TEST OUT THE WORRY. Set up a situation where your child can find out whether the worry is true or not. In Jo's story above, she and her mum made a mistake in the homework, on purpose. Jo went to school the next day to see what would happen.

d. After testing out the worry, have a nice chat about what happened. Did the worry come true? Did the teacher shout and hit? Did Jo cry and feel upset all day? Usually the answer is No, and your child has learnt an important lesson.

e. Give your child heaps and heaps of praise for being brave and testing out their worry. Maybe consider giving them a little reward too.

steps that you can take to help your child to test out their unrealistic worries.

Worry Time

Both adults and children alike need to learn to control their worries. However, this is easier said than done. Sometimes just pushing our worries away doesn't work – they just come back even worse than before. The reason for this is that, deep down, all worriers believe that they have to worry, or else something awful will happen.

Try the little quiz in Box 11.5.

I am willing to bet that you ticked yes to a few of those questions, even if you don't count yourself as a worrier. Well, we now know that children hold these sorts of beliefs as well. This is a bit of a problem. It means that whenever we push a worry away, a

Box 11.4. Dr Drusilla deals with worry

"Dear Dr Drusilla,

My little Kermit is a terrible worrier. He worries about everything all the time. He'll make himself go mad with worrying. What can I do?"

Kenneth Comberbatch, Great Collywobbles

Dr Drusilla replies:

"Dear Kenneth,

Fear not, for all this worrying may make Kermit sad, but it cannot make him go mad. Worrying is quite normal. Now, if you want to help Kermit to worry less, remember what I've said about listening to children's worries, about problem solving and about testing out worries. I'm sure if you do those things you will help Kermit to worry less. And remember Kenneth, children copy their parent's behaviour ... I wonder who he has learnt his worrying from ...?"

"Dear Dr Drusilla,

I did what you said and helped my Dora to test out her worries about going to parties. But Dr Drusilla, I found it SO hard. When I was sending her through the door she was crying and I felt so sorry for her that I had tears in my eyes too. I kept telling her to be careful, and be a brave girl, but it was all so horrible and I really don't think it worked."

Doris Dishcloth, Didsbury

Dr Drusilla replies:

"Dear Doris,

I think it's marvellous that you are pushing Dora to test out her worries. If you keep trying, it will work. But you are right, it is very hard for a caring mum to do. It is very easy for us to get upset as much as our children. But Doris, your little Dora will copy your behaviour. If you show that you are upset, she will be upset too. If you tell her she must be brave, she will think there really *must* be something to be scared of! My advice is calmly to send her off to the party with a smile and

Continued

> a wave, and a strict instruction to enjoy herself. Show her that you think it's all going to be fine. If you really don't think you can manage this, maybe you should get someone else to take her to the party. Hang in there Doris, she will thank you."

little voice, deep down, is saying, "but if you don't worry about this, everything will go disastrously wrong" or, "you are a bad person if you don't worry about this".

These sorts of beliefs are very difficult to change and so psychologists have devised a technique of getting round them. I call this technique 'worry time'. Using this technique, the worrier sets aside a short period of time each day (say 10–15 minutes). This is the same time every day, so it gets to be a good habit. During this time, the worrier can worry about any concerns that have popped into their head during the day. There are three really good reasons why worry time works:

Box 11.5. What do you think about worry?

Read the following statements, and tick any that you agree with:

	Yes	No
Worrying helps me to solve problems		
If I never worried, I would be less nice as a person		
Worrying helps me to spot difficulties in the future		
Worrying helps me to stay organised		
Worrying helps me to cope		
If I stopped worrying, things would start to fall apart		
There are some things that you *should* worry about		

1. During the day, when a worry pops up it becomes much easier to push it away if you know that you will definitely have time to deal with it later on. It means that those little beliefs like "I must worry about this to stay in control" don't get in the way. After all, you are not abandoning the worry, just postponing it a while.
2. By the time you get to 'worry time' some of the heat has often gone out of the worry. Time has passed, you are hopefully feeling a bit less stressed, the problem may even have gone away; and suddenly, the worry is much easier to deal with.
3. After a while, your brain gets really good at pushing away the worry and people who use this technique report that they start feeling more in control of their own mind.

Worry time has not been widely used with children – and there is very little research evidence to back it up. However, I use it with children, and so do a number of colleagues, and with the right support from parents we find that it works really well.

HOW TO DO WORRY TIME

- Pick a time in your child's day when you will be able to do 'worry time' with them. Choose a time when you are least likely to get interrupted by other people. It is best to make sure that the time is at least one hour before your child goes to bed.
- Tell your child to save all their worries for this time. If they have a worry during the day, they should not dwell on it there and then but save it for their 'worry time'.
- Each day, at this time, get together with your child and discuss any worries that they have had during the day. Use the techniques for unrealistic and realistic worries to deal with these worries.

- Give them lots of praise for postponing their worries to the worry time – maybe even consider a little reward if they have tried hard.
- Outside of worry time, try not to spend too much time talking to your child about their worries. Help them to distract themselves onto something else instead and give them praise and reward when they manage to do this. See 'withdrawing' below.
- However, if your child comes to you with a new worry that you have not discussed before, do not postpone this to worry time unless your child clearly indicates that they are happy to do this. With new worries, always give it a bit of time as soon as you possibly can.

Withdrawing

We have talked about how all children need attention from adults and they will get this any way that they can. In some families, children learn that they can only get attention by being outrageously naughty; in others they learn that they get it by being nice and doing kind things; in yet other families they learn that they get attention by being clever, or accomplished, or even by looking nice. All families are different, and we all have things that pluck our strings; and our kids learn this very, very early on.

Often with depressed or anxious kids, they have learnt that when they are upset they get attention from well-meaning parents. After all, it would have to be a hard parent who could ignore a distressed child ... wouldn't it ...?

The short answer to this question, of course, is "Yes"! The best parents are those who are tuned in to their child's mood and who react accordingly. However, we think that many anxious and depressed children have learnt that being upset is a shortcut to getting some of the fuss and reassurance that they need. This sounds terrible but I really don't mean it to. These children do not know that they are doing this, but at some subconscious level a little voice is saying, "I need some support and I know that my nice mum/dad/gran/teacher will come running if I get upset".

Throughout this book I have been talking about ways that your children can learn to get your attention by being brave, and nice, and sometimes for no reason at all – just because you love them. By now, hopefully most of this is in place and you are seeing some calming in your child. If this is the case, then I would suggest that you use the withdrawing technique that I talk about next. If you are not at this stage – if your child hasn't yet learnt to get the support and attention that they need in positive ways – then go back over those sections first. If you try the withdrawing technique and your child still *needs* to use their distress to get your attention and support, then it will not work.

THE WITHDRAWING TECHNIQUE

The withdrawing technique, essentially, means ignoring your child when they are worried or upset. This sounds very cruel, but read on as it should only be used in very specific circumstances when it is not cruel but is, instead, teaching your child to manage their own emotions.

WHEN TO USE THIS TECHNIQUE

Only use this technique in situations that you and your child have talked about and made plans for. So, for instance, if your child comes home from school in tears because of something that happened, don't ignore this. The first time that a child is distressed about something, you should make time to talk about this as soon as possible. You should then schedule a slot in your next 'worry time' to talk about it in detail and make a plan for dealing with it. Only use the withdrawal technique after you have spent some 'worry time' dealing with the issue and have decided what to do.

The next time the worry comes up say to your child, "we have talked about this, and we have decided what we are going to do". Check that they can remember the plan – but don't get into a big discussion about it. Tell your child that, if they like, you can talk it through again at their next worry time and then change the subject. If the child will not stop talking about the worry then you should try very hard to ignore this. Try to distract them onto something else. If necessary, start doing something else or leave the room.

You may find yourself getting a bit upset doing this – it is very hard to do. If you do get upset, remove yourself from the situation as it is really important that your child does not see you upset here.

The rules here are the same as for 'ignoring' (chapter 10). So, if you are not feeling strong, and know that you will end up giving in and talking about the worry, give in straight away. If you ignore for a while and then give in, you will be teaching your child that if they worry and are upset for long periods of time then they will get some attention.

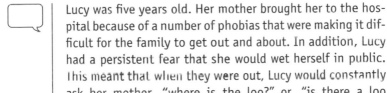

Lucy was five years old. Her mother brought her to the hospital because of a number of phobias that were making it difficult for the family to get out and about. In addition, Lucy had a persistent fear that she would wet herself in public. This meant that when they were out, Lucy would constantly ask her mother, "where is the loo?" or, "is there a loo nearby?" She also insisted on being taken to the loo about twice an hour when they were out. This made shopping trips exasperating for the family.

We knew that there wasn't anything physically wrong with Lucy and that she didn't actually need to go this often. When she was in the safety of her own home she only went to the loo every few hours. We decided that the problem was that Lucy's attention was very focussed on her bladder when she

Continued

was outside of the home. She was worried about wetting herself and so was paying close attention to feelings in her tummy. Unfortunately, because she was worried, this made her have funny feelings in her tummy. Even though she was only five years old, this bright little thing was interpreting the funny feelings as needing to go to the loo. We also decided that, because Mum always gave reassurance to Lucy – "yes Lucy, there is a loo over in the corner" – and took Lucy to the loo every half hour, Lucy was getting lots of attention and reassurance for her symptoms. We suspected that the reassurance was very motivating for Lucy and that this was actually making her symptoms worse. Lucy's mother was a very bright and psychologically-minded woman and instantly saw what the problem was. She came up with the solution on her own. She decided that she was not going to give Lucy this sort of reassurance any more. Instead, the next time they went out shopping she took Lucy to the loo before they left home and then explained that she would take her just once during the shopping trip – after an hour, when they would stop for a cup of tea – and then she would not be able to go again until they got home another hour later. She also told Lucy, very gently, that she would not be listening if Lucy asked where the nearest loo was. At first, according to Mum, things went really badly – Lucy asked where the loo was and because she got no answer she asked more and more and more. Lucy's mum thought she was going to have to give up on the experiment but, being a determined sort of person, she stuck at it. After about 20 minutes she noticed that Lucy started asking less. After half an hour Lucy stopped asking altogether and did not ask again for the whole trip.

Mum was amazed and thrilled that her experiment had worked. Moreover, she said that she didn't think that Lucy had just pushed her worries inside herself. Instead, because she was getting no attention and reassurance for her worrying, Mum thought that Lucy had actually *forgotten* to be worried. They had both had a lovely time shopping and had got many more trips planned.

Summary of Chapter Eleven

- Fears and worries are very common and, in themselves, can do no harm to your child.

➡ Fears

Fear is caused largely by two psychological processes:
- Avoidance – staying away from the feared object means that you never learn that it is OK.
- Fight or flight response – when we are scared our bodies get ready to run away which is why fear makes us feel so strange.

Treatment of fears works by *very gradually* introducing the child to the thing that they are scared of.

➡ Worries

Dealing with worry is more tricky, but there is much that parents can do:
- Realistic worries – problem solving with your child
- Unrealistic worries – helping your child to test out their worries
- Worry time – setting aside a regular short period when you will listen to your child's worries, so that they learn to keep some control over their worrying.

12

Facing facts

Whilst in most cases parents are not to blame for their child's anxiety or depression, the fact remains that there are some things that parents do that have a big effect on their children. In particular, there are two situations where we always suggest that families make special efforts to ensure that their behaviour does not harm their children, and when they should consider trying to get specialist help. These are when a parent has some psychological problems of their own, and when there is serious marital discord in the home. I will talk about each of these situations, suggesting where you can go for help, and what you can do to minimise the impact on your anxious or depressed child in the meantime.

Your own state of mind

If you have any psychological troubles yourself, whether these have been formally diagnosed or not, it is important to be aware of the ways that these problems can have an impact on your anxious or depressed child. I will list the main things that you need to watch out for. However, please do not worry. Just because you have difficulties of your own does not mean that you are a bad parent. The fact that you are reading this chapter suggests that you are aware that there might be an impact on your child, and that you are prepared to do something about it – this is the behaviour of a good, responsible parent – and always try to remember that nobody ever gets parenting right all of the time!

Negativity

If you yourself have mental health problems, whatever these may be, it is likely that you will spend some of your time feeling really quite down. Although you can't ever completely hide these feelings from your children, you can do a few things to make sure that your low mood doesn't spread around the home:

- Make sure that you still spend time having fun with your kids – even if you really, really don't feel like it.
- Try to avoid being snappy with your kids. Follow the guidance given in this book, and try, as much as you can, to stick to positive discipline.

Worrying and overprotection

If you are anxious or depressed, or sometimes if you have other types of mental health problem, you can find yourself feeling very nervous and jumpy. The world can feel like a very bad and dangerous place. Unfortunately, as we have seen in this book, for a child to get over their own anxiety/depression, they need to be getting strong signals that the world is a pretty safe place. If children believe that the world is a dangerous place, they will not want to go out and about and do all of the things that they need to do to get better. So, how can you make sure that your child doesn't pick up on your worries?

- Don't worry out loud in front of your kids. Kids learn their parents' worries really, really fast, especially if they are suffering from an anxiety disorder. If you have a lot of worries you may need to offload these to someone, but do try to find another adult rather than relying on your child. Some anxious kids, particularly, are very sensitive souls and can make great listening ears but, no matter how tempting, don't ever be tempted to use them as your own counsellor.
- Try not to overprotect your kids. As kids get older they want to do more and more things on their own. This striving for independence is a natural part of growing up. Anxious and depressed kids often need a bit of pushing to become independent and, as a parent, you are the best person to do this pushing. However, if you wrap your kids in cotton wool they won't get a chance to go out and learn that the world is basically fairly safe, and that people are pretty nice really, and all of the other confident thoughts that they need to learn. As well as not getting a chance to find out what the world is like, and what they can and can't cope with, children will read your overprotection as a sure sign that the world is too dangerous for them to cope with. If you are in doubt as to what you should and should not allow your kids to do, ask your child's teacher or ask other parents of children who are in the same class as your child. If more than half of the parents say it is OK for their child to do something, then be brave and let yours do it too.

Parental Fears and Avoidance

If you know that there are certain things that you can't do – perhaps because of your own anxiety or depression – consider whether these are things that may have an impact on your child. For example, if you are very shy and don't like socialising much, is this having an impact on your child's opportunities to learn social skills? Does your morbid fear of goldfish mean that you can't visit friends with fish tanks, running the risk that your child will soon think that goldfish are terrifying too? In all seriousness, kids do pick up fears from their parents really easily and, if parents are avoiding certain situations, they may be setting up a perfect scenario for their child to acquire the phobia too. There are two solutions to this problem – a good but hard one, and a slightly easier one. The tough one is to go and get some help to get over the fear yourself so that there is no risk that you will pass it onto your child. The easier one is to make sure that someone else in your child's life is giving them positive messages about the thing that you find scary, to cancel out the negative messages that you are giving. If you go for this second option, try to find someone close to your child (perhaps the other parent, or an aunt/older cousin, etc.) who isn't scared of the thing that you are scared of. Get them to spend some time with your child, doing the thing that you are terrified of (e.g. handling spiders, going out to crowded shopping centres). This way, your child will be learning that, just because you are scared of something, doesn't mean that it is scary for everyone. They will also be learning that they can cope with something that other people find tough, which will be good for their self esteem. Going back to the example where the parent is very shy – in this case, it would be wise for the parent to arrange for their child to have lots of opportunities for socialising outside of the home – e.g. by joining clubs, by being encouraged to visit friends' homes regularly, etc. You can do a lot to prevent your child from suffering in the way that you have.

If it gets really bad

If your own problems are quite severe – that is, if they are having an impact on what you can and can't do with your life or are having an impact on normal family life, then I would really strongly recommend that you go and get some help for yourself. Your GP will be able to refer you to see someone. If you decide to see someone privately, exercise caution, and follow the tips that are outlined in chapter 4. The sources of good therapists for children that are described in chapter 4 will also be good sources for a therapist for yourself.

Marital Discord

Whilst it is normal for families to have disagreements and to have times when they are annoyed with each other, if this is happening on a regular basis it can have a real impact on an anxious or depressed child. As a first step, I would strongly urge any parents experiencing serious marital discord to get some professional assistance as soon as possible.

Unfortunately, children do pick up on strains in their parents' relationship and it is hard to develop the Seven Confident Thoughts when you are living with unhappy parents. It is particularly important to go and seek urgent help if there is frequent, serious, arguing or *any* domestic violence, as this can have a very serious impact on children.

IN THE MEANTIME

In the meantime, the following tips should help to reduce the impact that these difficulties will have on your child:

- Try very, very hard to keep your arguments away from your children. Never, ever let an argument take place in earshot of the children. Also, just because the kids are upstairs, do not assume that they can't hear.
- Try very hard to keep up good co-parenting (see chapter 7). Avoid disagreeing about child-rearing in front of the children and try to back up the other parent's decisions, even if you don't agree with them.

SOURCES OF SUPPORT FOR FAMILIES FACING MARITAL DISCORD

Relate

Relate is a nationwide provider of relationship therapy and services. As well as providing individual therapy for couples wanting to improve their relationship, they can also provide telephone and online counselling. There is also counselling available for young people whose parents are separating.

Web: http://www.relate.org.uk

Tel: 0845 130 4016

Summary of Chapter Twelve

- There are two common family situations that can have a serious impact on the wellbeing of children – particularly those of a sensitive disposition. This chapter gives advice on how to minimise the impact on your children.

➡ Your own state of mind. If you are suffering from mental health difficulties, you should watch out for the following:

- Negativity towards your children
- Worrying and overprotection
- Teaching your children your own fears and avoidance

➡ Marital discord. If serious conflict is present in your home, this can have a real impact on your children. In this situation, you are advised to:

- Get help for you and your partner
- Avoid arguing in front of your children
- Keep up good co-parenting

13

What schools and teachers can do to help

Children spend a large proportion of their waking life at school, so what goes on there can have a real impact on their wellbeing. A good school can really help an anxious or depressed child to get over their difficulties.

The first thing to do is to talk to your child's school. Just knowing that your child is having some emotional problems may well trigger some helpful responses from school. Don't just assume that your child's teachers have noticed that there is a problem. Most teachers get very little training in spotting emotional difficulties in kids, and the research shows that even good teachers often do not spot problems such as these – not surprising when they have so many children to take care of. Likewise, most teachers have absolutely no training in how to deal with anxiety and depression, so they may well feel out of their depth. Do not feel embarrassed about sharing your knowledge of your child and their difficulties, and making suggestions that have helped you at home.

How to get school on your side

Talking to teachers can feel a bit intimidating – I still feel like a schoolgirl whenever I have to go and visit a school. However, things have moved on since we were at school and most teachers now welcome involvement from parents and are expected to treat parents' queries and comments with respect. So, even if you feel a bit anxious about doing it, do go and have a chat with school.

Teachers, however, are incredibly busy people and many of them are very stressed. It can be very difficult for them to make special arrangements for just one child. Do bear this in mind when you are asking for special help for your child. Just acknowledging that you know how busy they are and that you would like to negotiate what it is possible for them to do within the limited resources that they have available will help get you on their right side.

Who do I talk to?

If your child is in junior or infant school, the best person to approach to start with is probably their class teacher. Other good people to talk to are the school nurse, or the school special educational needs cordinator (SENCO).

If your child is in secondary school, the best person to start with is either the form teacher or the head of year. And, once again, other good people to talk to are the school nurse, or the school special educational needs coordinator (SENCO).

Once you have done this, they may suggest that the head of school or the head of year gets involved. Also, if they are not already involved, the school nurse or SENCO might get involved.

What do I tell them?

Just be open and honest and tell them all of the concerns that you have. If you have some concerns about how school are managing the problem, don't feel afraid to say this. However, try hard not come across as aggressive or complaining.

When going to schools, I always plan what I want to say in advance and try to have a clear idea of what I want to achieve in the meeting. This way, we can get through the meeting quickly (always viewed positively by teachers) and come out with some concrete decisions made.

Working with any large organisation such as a school can sometimes be frustrating. Most schools have very few staff to deal with very many children and teachers are often stressed and overworked. Sometimes it feels as if things don't happen as quickly or as easily as they should. In these circumstances it is very easy to get annoyed, and tempting to make a stroppy phone call to the head teacher. Although this feels like a good vent for emotions at the time, it almost always has very negative consequences in the long run. In my experience, the parents who get the best out of schools are the ones who are persistent and determined, but who also do all of their talking with a smile on their face. Teachers are like anyone else: they will bend to a bit of pressure but are much more likely to do this for someone they like and feel warm towards. So, even if you get really annoyed with school, put down that telephone! Wait until you are a bit calmer before you call.

As I've already said, most teachers get almost no training in matters relating to children's mental health. So, although they clearly know children very well and many respond to children's problems with really good, practical, common sense, many will not have a clue how they should deal with an anxious or depressed child. If your child has been referred to a mental health professional, ask this professional to give school a call, to give some advice. If that is not possible or more advice is needed, consider giving school this book to read, or give them the summaries at the end of each chapter. Chapters 8, 9, and 10 are most relevant for schools.

In addition, the next section gives some practical tips on steps that schools can take to help an anxious or depressed child or adolescent.

Practical steps that school can take

POSITIVE DISCIPLINE

The most useful thing that a school can do is make sure that it is a positive, happy place for children to be. Schools can do a lot to foster the Seven Confident Thoughts in children (see Box 7.1 on page 59). However, to do this they need to be places that are relatively calm, predictable, and fair. Most schools now attempt to achieve this and do so by using positive discipline such as that described in this book. Schools should be focussing on rewarding positive behaviour before they attempt to reduce negative

---

Box 13.1. Positive Discipline for schools

- School staff watch out for good behaviour and give good clear praise when they see it.
- School staff decide on a type of good behaviour that they really want to encourage (e.g. trying hard at schoolwork, acts of kindness, etc.) and reward these using stickers or other small prizes.
- The rules about bad behaviour are clear to all – parents, teachers, support staff and, of course, the children. Everyone knows what behaviour is not allowed.
- Everyone knows what will happen if negative behaviour is seen.
- Punishments for unwanted behaviour are:
  - not too severe
  - understood by everyone
  - consistently applied
  - given out as soon as possible
- Once a punishment is out of the way, the unwanted behaviour is forgotten about.

behaviour using punishment. If punishment is used (and in reality, it is going to be needed sometimes in all schools), then they should follow the rules given in chapter 10 of this book.

ENCOURAGING CHILDREN TO TAKE PART

Both anxious and depressed children really benefit from taking part in lots of social activities even if they don't feel like it. School is a great source of opportunities for this. Teachers and other school staff such as playground and lunchtime supervisors can be real allies for the parent who wants to get their kid engaging in more social activities.

Explain to school why social activities are so good for your child (see chapter 6 for a reminder) and ask them to lend a hand in getting your child active at school. They can do this by keeping an eye out for your child. If they spot your child standing in a corner doing nothing, ask them to suggest some activities to your child, and, especially for younger children, pair them up with a friendly and helpful child who can chivvy them into activities.

BEING FIRM BUT KIND ABOUT AVOIDANCE

There are many school-based activities that anxious and depressed children find very hard. Based on the children that I have seen, I would say that the following activities are the most likely to cause them problems:

- Assemblies
- Lunchtime
- P.E./games
- Lessons that they struggle with (e.g. maths, French).
- Tasks that require public speaking e.g. reading out aloud, debates, school plays

As we saw in chapter 11, avoiding activities that feel unpleasant causes big problems in the long run and children should be encouraged to face up to the activities if they can. If your child has developed a real phobia of these activities, just forcing them to take part may not be the right way to go. In this situation, talk to your therapist, or follow the guidance for fear hierarchies in chapter 11. However, if your child hasn't got a phobia of the situation and just finds it very unpleasant, it is best to encourage them to take part as much as they can. Of course, when your child is trying to avoid something at home, you will be on hand to encourage them to face their fear but, at school, you will not be. In this case you will be relying on the teachers to do the job for you. If you know that your child tries to avoid a particular part of school life, ask the teacher to:

- Watch for the child trying to avoid the activity: many kids will do this by complaining that they don't feel very well; others will simply not show up.
- If the child tries to avoid the activity, firmly – but calmly and kindly – tell them that they need to take part, even if they don't feel well.
- Once the child has taken part in the activity, ask the teacher to give the child praise for coping well. For older children, this needs to be done very discreetly, so as not to embarrass the adolescent in front of their peers. For younger children, a little reward might also help. If school doesn't have a box of little rewards to use for good behaviour, ask the teacher to discreetly give out rewards that you have provided. If school are not happy with providing rewards for just one child, get them to give your child a sticker which he/she can trade in for a little reward from you later in the day.
- If the child refuses to take part in the activity, they should never be punished for this. However, they should always be given an alternative activity to do. This alternative activity is to make sure that they don't get to use this spare time to do something nice, which would act as a reward for their

avoidance. Ask the teacher to find an activity for your child to do while they are avoiding. This activity should be as boring as humanly possible. Since you will know your child better than the teacher, you could suggest something that you know your child will find intensely boring. For instance, one child might find placing piles of exercise books in alphabetical order intensely boring, whilst another might find it quite pleasing. Liaise with the teacher to make sure that time spent avoiding one activity does not end up being fun! Depending on the child, they may need to be supervised whilst doing this, but try to make sure that this supervision does not end up being a nice cosy chat with the friendly school secretary! Remember, any time spent avoiding an activity should be made to be really, really boring.

CLEAR AND REASONABLE EXPECTATIONS FOR PUPILS' ACADEMIC PERFORMANCE

Schools can be fantastic for raising your depressed or anxious child's self esteem. There is so much scope in school for mastering new skills, and achieving targets. However, whether these are translated into boosts to your child's self esteem depends, to some extent, on how this is managed by your child's school.

CLEAR GOALS

The best schools have clear goals for children. The kids know what the goals are, and they know when they have achieved them. When they do achieve, the kids get loads of praise for this. Check whether this is happening in your child's school. Does your child know what each teacher expects of him/her? This can be as simple as knowing what is expected of homework, but may extend to knowing what SATS level they are aiming for at the end of the year.

MANAGEABLE GOALS

It might be a good idea to check that the levels expected of your child are reasonable. Expectations should be tailored to each child and, if your child is depressed, and sometimes if severely anxious, these expectations should be reduced for the time being – lots of research shows that it is difficult to do as well as normal at schoolwork when you are struggling with mental health problems. If your child's school are not aware of this, please do tell them to be prepared for poorer academic performance from your child until the problems are sorted out.

COMMUNICATING SUCCESS TO PUPILS

Even when high academic standards are met, not all schools are good at communicating this success to children. This a particular problem for depressed and anxious kids as they can be prone to comparing themselves too much with other children. One anxious and depressed teenager that I saw thought that he was doing badly because some of the very bright teenagers in his grammar school were getting straight As. He didn't seem to notice that his string of good passes in every subject was a sign that he was doing as well as expected and more besides. A little chat with his form teacher ensured that he got more praise for his good performance, and his self esteem soon began to lift.

GO FOR 'HEALTHY SCHOOLS' STATUS

'Healthy Schools' is a government initiative to make schools healthier places – not just physically healthier, but socially and emotionally healthier too. Schools do not have to apply for 'healthy school' status, but if they do they will be given help to implement lots of different programmes that will be of real benefit to all pupils, and especially to your anxious or depressed child! A 'Healthy School' needs to prove that it looks after its pupils' emotional needs by, amongst other things, having a clear and sensible anti-bullying policy, and a policy for rewarding and encouraging positive behaviour. Many 'Healthy Schools' will introduce an activity called 'circle time' where children sit round with their teacher and talk about emotional issues in a way that is appropriate for their age. Coping with life's little problems is discussed and the intention is that children can be more open about difficulties that they are facing at school and will learn new ways of dealing with these. As well as this, schools can choose from a menu of activities and policies that they will implement to enhance the emotional wellbeing of children (and staff too!). If your child's school is not a 'Healthy School', talk to the head teacher and, if that fails, the governors, about applying to join this initiative.

What about bullying?

Dealing with bullying is a complex area, and well beyond the scope of this book. If you fear that your child is being bullied, a good place to start for advice is Kidscape or Childline.

KIDSCAPE

This a national organisation set up to help parents and organisations who look after children, such as schools, deal with the problem of bullying. They have an excellent website with advice for parents, and masses of resources and information for schools. There is a helpline for parents (number below), and they run confidence-building courses for children who have been bullied. Kidscape will send trainers to schools to give workshops on how to prevent and deal with bullying.
Tel: 08451 205 204
Website: http://www.kidscape.org.uk/

CHILDLINE/NSPCC

Childline is in the process of merging with the NSPCC, but their mission will stay the same. If your child is being bullied he/she can contact Childline for a confidential chat to an advisor with expertise in this area. The Childline website has a range of resources for teachers who want to help prevent and manage bullying in their schools.

Tel: 0800 1111

Website: http://www.childline.org.uk/

Who to talk to if school are unhelpful

In the event that you feel that your child's school is being very unhelpful, or is actively doing something that is feeding into your child's anxiety or depression, there are several steps that you can take.

TALK TO THE HEAD TEACHER

If you haven't already done this, do go and talk to the head teacher about your concerns. Do try to talk calmly. If you are not satisfied with the response that you get, ask the head teacher for the contact details of the chair of the school governors.

TALK TO THE GOVERNORS

Once you have exhausted all avenues by talking directly to school, the next step is to talk to the governors. The contact details for the chair of the school governors should be on the school website. Also, the school office should be able to give you this information, as should the local education authority. The governors are a group of people who are recruited to make sure that the school is run well. Some of the governors will be school staff, but some will be parents of children at the school, and yet others will be community governors who do not have any relationship with the school. There should also be a representative of the local education authority. The governors form an independent body, and decisions that they take must be followed by the school. The governors should have a 'complaints' committee that deals with any complaints that are raised by parents of children at the school.

LOCAL EDUCATION AUTHORITY (LEA)

If you are unhappy with the response that you get from the school governors, the next port of call is the local education authority (LEA). The LEA governs all state schools. The phone number will be online and is usually in the telephone directories. In some areas of the country, there are voluntary agencies that are set up to help parents to negotiate with schools; it is worth asking the LEA if any such services are available in your area.

SPECIAL SHORT-TERM UNITS FOR VULNERABLE CHILDREN

In many Local Education Authorities, there are special units where vulnerable children can be offered education in the short-term. If your child is offered a place in one of these units, please do work very hard to get them there. The units that I have known have been universally wonderful. They generally have very small numbers of pupils and will only take children who are fairly well behaved (so there is little risk of disruption or bullying in the classroom). The staff who choose to work in such schools are usually especially warm and dedicated people and I have seen some very troubled children flourish in such settings. However, in most cases, these units are only intended for short-term use. They are not meant to provide for a child's entire education. Instead, the staff will work to raising a child's confidence levels to the point where they are ready to go back into mainstream education – back to their old school, or if needs be, a different one.

HOME EDUCATION – A LAST RESORT

In desperation, some families resort to educating their child at home instead of going to school. However, for anxious or depressed children, this is rarely a good solution in the long term. Indeed, I have seen a number of children who have been taken out of school, who, after the initial relief, have gone downhill rapidly. I would caution any parent against taking this drastic step without exhausting every other option first. Depressed and anxious kids desperately need lots of social contact with other children, and they need to be kept busy. It is difficult for even the most dedicated parent to meet these needs entirely on their own. Think about the Seven Confident Thoughts (Box 7.1 on page 59) and how home education would impact on these.

A final note – how can you help school to help your child?

KEEP THEM POSTED

Do communicate with school. They can only help your child if they know that there is a problem, and know what to do.

KEEP DROP-OFFS CALM AND TEAR FREE

Bringing up an anxious or depressed child is a big strain on a parent's emotions. When your child is crying or distressed, it is easy to become upset yourself. School drop-off time is a real flash point for these emotions. However, if you can cover up your own distress then your child will cope much better. If your child starts crying, try not to join in! Instead, give them a big smile, tell them to have a lovely day, and shove them through the door, before retiring to your car with a box of tissues.

AVOID COMPLAINING ABOUT SCHOOL IN FRONT OF YOUR CHILD

Sometimes schools do things that don't help and, if so, you need to vent your frustration about this. However, I would strongly urge you to do this when your child is well out of earshot. As we discussed in previous chapters, children copy their parents and easily take on their parents' opinions. If your child knows that you don't have confidence in the school, then they will lose confidence too. This is a slippery slope to go down. Once the child loses confidence in their school, it becomes very difficult for the parents to convince them that it is a safe and happy place for them to go.

Summary of Chapter Thirteen

➡ Parents should talk to school. They may not know there is a problem and, even if they do, will have had little training in what they can do to help

➡ Practical steps that you can encourage schools to take:

   ➡ Use positive discipline

   ➡ Encourage kids to take part in activities

   ➡ Discourage avoidance

   ➡ Set clear, reasonable expectations for pupils

• What to do if school are unhelpful:

   ➡ Talk to the head teacher/governers/LEA

   ➡ Home education – this should be an absolutely last resort

➡ How you can help school to help your child:

   ➡ Keep them posted

   ➡ Avoid tearful drop-offs

   ➡ Avoid complaining about school in front of your child

14

Rounding up

I hope that this book has helped you to cope with your child's difficulties. However, if you are still having problems after reading it and trying to implement some of the advice that I have given you, then I would urge you to go and get some professional help for your child.

Even if your child is doing well, it is important to be aware that everyone has symptoms of anxiety and depression from time to time. We have blue patches, or times when we have a lot of worries. This is normal and you should not panic when this happens to your child.

However, at the same time, it is important to be aware that a child who has been anxious or depressed once is more vulnerable to having the same difficulties again. In order to minimise the chance of a relapse, it is a good idea to keep going with all of the skills that you have learnt to apply. Do not forget to keep giving your child loads of positive attention for good, confident behaviours. Do not forget to use positive discipline, such as mild consequences and time out when they produce behaviours that you cannot tolerate. Above all, do not give up on spending positive, quality time with them on a daily basis. All children need this, and your child needs it more than most.

If your child does start to slip back into old ways, they need you to be upbeat. Do not allow yourself to be dragged down with them. They need you to have the confidence that you can beat the problems again. Go back to the skills in this book and make sure that you are applying them consistently. Give your child the message that between you, you will get them through this again.

Appendix

Activity Chart

	Monday	Tuesday	Wednesday	Thursday	Friday	Saturday	Sunday
7am–8am							
8am–9am							
9am–10am							
10am–11am							
11am–Noon							
Noon–1pm							
1pm–2pm							
2pm–3pm							
3pm–4pm							
4pm–5pm							
5pm–6pm							
6pm–7pm							
7pm–8pm							
8pm–9pm							
9pm–10pm							

Activity Chart

	Monday	Tuesday	Wednesday	Thursday	Friday	Saturday	Sunday
7am–8am							
8am–9am							
9am–10am							
10am–11am							
11am–Noon							
Noon–1pm							
1pm–2pm							
2pm–3pm							
3pm–4pm							
4pm–5pm							
5pm–6pm							
6pm–7pm							
7pm–8pm							
8pm–9pm							
9pm–10pm							

Activity Chart

	Monday	Tuesday	Wednesday	Thursday	Friday	Saturday	Sunday
7am–8am							
8am–9am							
9am–10am							
10am–11am							
11am–Noon							
Noon–1pm							
1pm–2pm							
2pm–3pm							
3pm–4pm							
4pm–5pm							
5pm–6pm							
6pm–7pm							
7pm–8pm							
8pm–9pm							
9pm–10pm							

STAR CHART

This star chart belongs to:

I will get a star every time that I:

When I have got................stars, I will get a treat.

My treat is.................

Index

Note: page references in *italics* indicate material in text boxes.

COPING WITH BIPOLAR DISORDER

Steven Jones, Peter Hayward & Dominic Lam
1–85168–299–6 * paperback * £10.99

Coping With Bipolar Disorder draws on the combined expertise of three leading specialists to offer a comprehensive and practical guide to living with the symptoms and effects of bipolar disorder (manic depression).

Designed specifically for sufferers of bipolar disorder, their carers, friends and family, this indispensable handbook combines comprehensive information on the condition and available treatments with a new approach that encourages patients to manage their own psychological health using cognitive behavioural therapy, as well as the more traditional medication regimes. The result is a straightforward and readable book that will empower sufferers, in addition to giving them necessary advice on such key issues as sleep habits, coping with stress and anger, and relating to family and friends.

With real-life case studies, helpful chapter summaries, and a full list of support organizations and web groups, this guide will both inform and empower all those who live with the bewildering turbulence of bipolar disorder.

Steven Jones is Reader in Clinical Psychology at the University of Manchester, Academic Division of Clinical Psychology, Wythenshawe Hospital, Manchester, UK, and Honorary Consultant Clinical Psychologist at Pennine Care Trust, UK.

Peter Hayward is a Consultant Clinical Psychologist at the South London and Maudsley NHS Trust in London, and an Honorary Senior Lecturer at the Institute of Psychiatry, London, UK.

Dominic Lam is Professor of Clinical Psychology at the University of Hull, UK

'If ever a book lived up to its title, this is it. The clear strategies, tools and techniques presented here with such understanding should make all the difference to those living with Bipolar Disorder – highly recommended.'

STEPHEN FRY

'This is an excellent book ... well-written, comprehensive, practical, wise and empowering.'

DR PETER KINDERMAN, Professor of Clinical Psychology,
University of Liverpool

'This book is practical, realistic, and well focused, emphasizing the individual, family and social resources that can and should be used to deal with a condition as complex as bipolar disorder. Patients and families will undoubtedly benefit from reading this volume.'

Quarterly Journal of Mental Health

COPING WITH SCHIZOPHRENIA

Steven Jones & Peter Hayward

1–85168–344–5 * paperback * £12.99

Specifically designed for people with a diagnosis of schizophrenia, their caregivers, friends and family, *Coping with Schizophrenia* is an empowering book that sensitively combines factual information and advice with encouragement.

Drawing on the very latest research, as well as their own extensive clinical experience, Doctors Jones and Hayward present the facts of the condition, including definitions and symptoms, the truth (or not) behind common myths, advice on dealing with professionals, medication and its effectiveness, the benefits of cognitive therapy, and much, much more. The result is a uniquely informative and positive book that covers an enormous range of issues and offers those living with schizophrenia the opportunity to play a decisive role in managing and maintaining their own well-being.

Steven Jones is Reader in Clinical Psychology at the University of Manchester, Academic Division of Clinical Psychology, Wythenshawe Hospital, Manchester, UK, and Honorary Consultant Clinical Psychologist at Pennine Care Trust, UK.

Peter Hayward is a Consultant Clinical Psychologist at the South London and Maudsley NHS Trust in London, and an Honorary Senior Lecturer at the Institute of Psychiatry, London, UK.

'*Coping With Schizophrenia* is a practical, helpful guide on the path toward recovery. It confronts difficult issues in ways that both empower individuals and provide hope for the journey. It offers tools and shared experiences that can help reduce isolation – reassuring people living with the illness and the people who love them that they are not alone.'

> **KEN DUCKWORTH**, Medical Director, NAMI (National Alliance for the Mentally Ill), USA

'A sympathetic and sensible book, which not only removes much of the fear, loneliness and stigma that surround schizophrenia, but gives up-to-date information and a fascinating overview. It also gives practical encouragement to those faced with such a diagnosis, and their families will find here new strategies and therapies with which to combat this cruel illness and survive.'

> **MARJORIE WALLACE**, Founder and Chief Executive of SANE, UK

'This is an excellent book [and] will make a very significant contribution to helping those with a diagnosis of schizophrenia. The book is extremely well written and achieves the difficult feat of combining optimism with realism.'

> **DAVID R. HEMSLEY**, Professor of Abnormal Psychology, Consultant Clinical Psychologist, Institute of Psychiatry, King's College London